UPSTAIRS, DOWNSTAIRS

Did Jesus Want a Two–Class Church?

"If you had known what this means, 'I desire mercy, and not sacrifice'." (Matt. 12:7)

Dedicated to laypeople in the Church

UPSTAIRS, DOWNSTAIRS

Did Jesus Want a Two-Class Church?

HERBERT HAAG

Translated by
Robert Nowell

A Crossroad Book
The Crossroad Publishing Company
New York

This translation first published in the U.S.A. in 1998 by
THE CROSSROAD PUBLISHING COMPANY
370 Lexington Avenue
New York, NY 10017

This translation first published in Great Britain in 1998 by
BURNS & OATES
Wellwood, North Farm Road,
Tunbridge Wells, Kent TN2 3DR

Original edition
Worauf es ankommt. Wollte Jesus eine Zwei-Stände-Kirche?
Published by Verlag Herder
Freiburg im Breisgau, 1997

Library of Congress Cataloging-in-Publication Data
Haag, Herbert, 1915-
    [Worauf es ankommt? English]
    Upstairs, downstairs : did Jesus want a two-class church? /
Herbert Haag : translated by Robert Nowell
        p.   cm.
    Includes bibliographical references.
    ISBN 0-8245-1752-0 (pbk.)
    1. Catholic Church—Clergy—History of doctrines. 2. Priesthood—
History of doctrines—Early church, ca. 30-600. 3. Clergy—Office—
History of doctrines—Early church, ca.30-600. I. Title.
BX1912.H22   1998
262'.02—dc21   98-11889
                                                            CIP

1 2 3 4 5 6 7 8 9 10   02 01 00 99 98

Typeset by Search Press Limited
Printed in Finland by Werner Söderström Oy

Contents

Foreword

The crisis of the Roman Catholic priesthood is manifest. Whatever the official Church has undertaken so far to meet it has remained without effect. The shortage of priests, communities deprived of the eucharist, celibacy, the ordination of women—these indicate the problems which to a considerable extent, though not exclusively, define the present troubles of the Catholic Church. More and more frequently laypeople are installed as leaders of congregations but, because they have not been "ordained," are unable to celebrate the eucharist with their congregation even though this is something they would properly be obliged to do. In the early Church this was not a problem. Then the celebration of the eucharist was solely in the control of the congregation. Those who, in agreement with the congregation, presided at it were not "ordained" but ordinary members of the congregation. Today we would call them laypeople: men, but also women, usually married, but also unmarried. What was decisive was the commission given them by the congregation. Why should what was possible then not be possible today?

If, as is claimed, Jesus established the priesthood of the New Covenant, why is nothing of this to be perceived during the first four centuries of the Church's history? Beyond this, all the seven sacraments recognized by the Catholic Church are supposed to have been founded by Jesus. Proving this is difficult in the case of more than one sacrament, and when it comes to the sacrament of order it is downright impossible. Rather Jesus showed by what he said and by what he did that he did not want any priests. He himself was not a priest, nor was any of the Twelve, nor Paul.

Still less is it possible to trace the office of bishop back to Jesus. The assumption that in order to ensure the continuation of their office the apostles installed bishops as their successors is untenable. Like every other office in the Church the office of bishop is a creation of the Church: it developed historically. And for this reason these two offices of bishop and priest are at any time at the Church's free disposal. They can be retained, altered, or done away with.

The Church's crisis will continue for as long as it does not decide to give itself a new constitution in which there is no longer any place for two classes—priests and laypeople, ordained and non-ordained—but a commission from the Church is sufficient to lead a congregation and to celebrate the eucharist with it. And such a commission can be bestowed on men and women, the married and the unmarried. Thus at one stroke the problem of the ordination of women and the question of celibacy are both solved.

To the demand that there should not be two classes in the Church the objection will above all be raised that there have always been organic developments which can only indirectly be grounded in the New Testament. Infant baptism is cited as an example. It cannot be referred explicitly to the New Testament, but at the same time it does not contradict it. However, reference to developments is tenable only to the extent that these are in agreement with the gospel's fundamental statements. If on decisive points they contradict these, they are illegitimate, insufferable, and harmful.

This quite certainly applies to the priestly Church. An examination of the biblical and early Christian evidence shows unequivocally and convincingly that hierarchy and priesthood developed in the Church through bypassing scripture and were later justified dogmatically as belonging to it. All the indications point to the hour having struck for the Church to think again and return to its real nature.

My profound thanks are due to Katharina Elliger and Margot Höfling for preparing the typescript, and to my colleagues Meinrad Limbeck, Willy Rordorf, Otto Wermelinger and Dietrich Wiederkehr for their professional help and advice. Ludger Hohn-Kemler has, as always, carried out his task as editor in exemplary fashion. I can only express my admiration for the distinguished services of the Lucerne Central Library and the helpfulness of their loan department.

Among the dedicatees of this book I should single out the Catholics of those dioceses where my immediate ministry was served: Chur, Basle, and Rottenburg-Stuttgart.

Lucerne, New Year's Day 1997
Herbert Haag

CHAPTER I

The "Discovery" of the Laity

The twentieth century, we are told, is the century of the laity, the century in which the Church has "discovered" the laity: this is the emphatic way in which the change that has come about in the Church in our time is evaluated. But if this is so it beggars understanding. For what are the laity other than Jesus' disciples (of both sexes) or, as they were called from a very early age (Acts 11:26), Christians?[1] On this view it took the Christian Church two thousand years to discover Christians! People talk too of the "awakening" of the laity, of their "coming of age," of the "hour of the laity" having struck. But in that case what were the laity in the preceding nineteen centuries?

As we shall see (see pp. 100ff. below), the laity emerges as a "class" with the formation from the third century onward of a hierarchy, of an "order of priests," of a clergy, after the previous multiplicity of ministries in the congregations had been channelled into the classic threefold office of bishop, presbyter and deacon (see pp. 98–100f. below). With this the devaluation of the laity also set in. To begin with, the distinction between office-holders and non-office-holders may have been kept within bounds. But soon it was to be intensified by the fact that taking on an office was made dependent upon receiving ordination. Henceforth the ordained and the non-ordained, *ordo* and *plebs*,

---

1. The words "lay," "laity" derive from the Greek *laos*, people. In ecclesiastical language the laity are those who belong to the "people" as distinguished from the clergy. As we shall see (p. 84 below), the word "lay" appears for the first time in Christian literature in 1 Clement (dating from the end of the first century). However, what the word denotes in that context is the body of Jewish believers in contrast to the priests and Levites of the Temple. By the start of the third century the term has been transferred to the Christian believer. The layperson is now the ordinary Christian in contrast to the priest or deacon (Clement of Alexandria), to the cleric (Origen), to the office-holder (Tertullian): see Peter Neuner, *Der Laie und das Gottesvolk*, Frankfurt-am-Main 1988, pp. 42–5.

stood over against each other as two classes divided not only by their role in worship but also socially.[2] The distinction between *ordo* and *plebs*, clergy and laity, became the decisive characteristic of the Church, and this has persisted until today.

From now on the layperson is the non-priest or non-cleric. "He or she is now defined by not belonging to the class of the clergy."[3]

Various developments have contributed to the gulf between clergy and laity becoming deeper and deeper. Two above all deserve mention. The first was the Constantinian revolution, the granting of privileged status to the Christian Church by the Roman emperor Constantine and its incorporation in the State (from AD 312 onward). With this the distinction between élite and subordinates which the State took for granted spread to the

---

2. On this subject cf. especially Alois Sustar, "Der Laie in der Kirche," in J. Feiner (ed.), *Fragen der Theologie heute*, Einsiedeln 1960, pp. 519-48.

3. Neuner, *op. cit.* p. 45. The Churches of the Reformation also talk of laypeople. But because they do not recognize clergy as such the concept of layperson must have another meaning than that of the non-cleric. In Protestantism the "layperson" is contrasted on the one hand with the person who is theologically educated, on the other with the person who, although not theologically educated, is engaged full-time in the Church's ministry. In contrast to this latter kind of "layperson," the first category, the ordinary members of the congregation, are occasionally referred to as the "genuine" laity (Gerhard Grohs and Gernot Czell [ed.], *Kirche in der Welt—Kirche der Laien?*, Frankfurt-am-Main 1990, p. 8). It would be surprising if the same kind of tensions between these various groups did not exist in the Protestant world as in the Catholic. "It seems as if the laity have had great difficulty in being appropriately involved in internal Church decisions. . . . So within the Evangelical Churches there has developed a dangerous division of congregation members according to how close they are to the Church's ministry or distant from it" (ibid. p. 9). There is thus no lack of Protestant studies of the "office of the laity in Church and theology" (such as, besides the volume by Grohs and Czell referred to above Henning Schröer and Gerhard Müller [ed.], *Vom Amt des Laien in Kirche und Theologie. Festschrift f²r Gerhard Krause*, Berlin 1982).

(In the English-speaking world the situation is more complex. Even in a Calvinist Church such as the Church of Scotland there is a clear distinction between ministers and elders on the one hand, who govern the Church through the three layers of Church courts—kirk session, presbytery, and general assembly—and ordinary Church members. The Church of England and other Anglican Churches have a very strong notion of clergy and in many ways can seem more clericalized than the Roman Catholic Church.—*Trans.*)

Church.[4] "What linked hierarchy and laity together receded more and more into the background, what divided them was emphasized more and more."[5]

The Reformation intensified this tendency. It rejected the hierarchy and the ministerial priesthood and thus provoked the old Church to insist on these all the more strongly. In post-Tridentine theology this led to Church and hierarchy being equated and ecclesiology turning into "hierarchology."[6] By "Church" people now understood pope, bishops, and priests, or a curial "magisterium"—in brief, what today we call the "official Church." This idea has persisted into our own time. It is reflected even in hymns in current use.

1: Laborious beginnings

A fundamental re-appraisal became noticeable in the official Church only in the twentieth century.[7] It is linked with Pius XI, pope from 1922 to 1939, and his encouragement of Catholic Ac-

---

4. "With the 'Christianization' of these structures (*i.e.* of the Roman State) that began under Constantine the danger admittedly arose of relying more on the system to win people over" (Peter Stockmeier, "Evangelisierung in der frühen Kirche," in H. Erharter and R. Schwarzenberger (ed.), *Kirche in gemeinsamer Verantwortung*, Vienna 1987, pp. 59-74, here p. 72).

5. Sustar, *op. cit.* p. 524.

6. Sustar, *op. cit.* p. 525.

7. This does not exclude the existence of previous successful efforts toward the emancipation of the laity. André Vauchez (*Les laïcs au Moyen Age. Pratiques et expériences religieuses*, Paris 1987) talks of an "awakening of the laity" that took place in the period between the eleventh and thirteenth centuries, and he sums the development up as follows: "In the twelfth and thirteen centuries, as we have seen, there took place an undeniable rehabilitation of the lay state. This period saw the disappearance of a series of blockages and restrictions that formed an obstacle to ordinary Catholics gaining access to an authentic religious life. The first concerned war: it was first regulated and then blessed by the Church in the context of the Crusades; the second referred to manual work, of which the ascetic worth and above all the social usefulness were appreciated more and more positively by the clergy, whether it was a question of the work of peasants, of artisans, or even of merchants. Of these some hagiographers and theologians, for the most part from the ranks of the mendicant Orders, did not hesitate to maintain, at the beginning of the fourteenth century, that they could attain holiness in the exercise of their profession. For all these men, and for women as well, the practice of charity through works of mercy offered another

tion. Admittedly already in the second half of the nineteenth century, first of all in Italy, organizations and associations had arisen with the explicit aim of defending the rights of the Church.[8] The year 1890 saw the foundation of the *Volksverein für das katholische Deutschland* (People's Association for Catholic Germany)[9], and 1904 saw the foundation on the same model of the *Schweizerische Katholische Volksverein* (Swiss Catholic People's Association) with its headquarters in Lucerne.[10] All associations of this kind understood themselves more as defenders of the clerical Church than advocates of the laity. Thus the historian Karl Otmar von Aretin writes of the Catholic Action brought into being by Pius XI: "The aim of this organization was to activate the laity, but it contributed more to the building up of papal absolutism than to bringing about the independence of the laity."[11]

Catholic Action was Pius XI's favourite child. He defined it as "the co-operation and participation of the laity in the Church's

---

opportunity of working out their salvation, while penitential spirituality gave weight to humility, self-denial and poverty. It is a period when the canonists acknowledged the existence of a new type of Christian, the 'religious layman' (*laicus religiosus*), neither worldly nor a recluse but striving to live according to the demands of the gospel in his professional and family life. Even the fundamental obstacle which sexuality had formed until then, preventing married people and women above all from attaining holiness, seems to become softened during the thirteenth century with the elaboration of the new concept of conjugal chastity" (pp.288-9).

To this context belong also the Béguines, the twelfth-century movement with its overtones of female emancipation that developed its own form of the religious life independent of existing monastic patterns and aroused the mistrust and suspicion of the clerical Church precisely because of its originality and independence.

8. Konrad Algermissen, *s.v.* "Katholische Aktion," in *Lexikon für Theologie und Kirche* (LTK), Freiburg-im-Breisgau 1933, vol. 5, cols 902-8, here 903-4.

9. LTK 1933, vol. 10, cols 681-2,[2] 1957-65, cols 860-1.

10. Cf. J. Meier, *Der Schweizerische Katholische Volksverein in seinem Werden und Wirken*, Lucerne 1954 (including the nineteenth-century prehistory).

11. *Papsttum und moderne Welt*, Munich 1970, p. 187. Agreeing with this is A. Stoecklin, *Schweizer Katholizismus*, Zürich 1978, with evidence showing that the urgent task of Catholic Action was seen to lie in educating the political conscience. H. Kühner (*Das Imperium der Päpste*, Zürich 1977, p. 379) attributes a judgment virtually identical with that of Aretin to the Munich Church historian G. Schwaiger, but without citing any reference.

hierarchical apostolate."[12] In other words, the Church's apostolate, its active witness to what Jesus proclaimed, ought not to be or remain the exclusive province of the hierarchy. Laypeople too should make their contribution to it. In this way they appear as assistants in the service of the hierarchy. They should be at hand at the command or even whim of the hierarchy (*"ut ad nutum hierarchiae ecclesiasticae praesto sint"*).[13] The way in which they organize themselves needs the agreement of the hierarchy. "Hierarchy" and "holy orders" remain the key concepts even in the age of Catholic Action.

One of the leading experts on that period summarizes the consequences for Germany as follows: "In Germany its special tasks needed to lie in guiding into a joint social apostolate the flourishing network of organizations that had developed in the Catholic movement of previous decades, and doing this through standardization, closer integration into the hierarchy, and stricter central control."[14] So the change brought about by Catholic Action in distinction to previous lay activity should be seen predominantly in its closer links with the hierarchy.[15]

Under Pius XII, pope from 1939 to 1958, Catholic Action as it had been understood by Pius XI was to experience the cor-

---

12. Jacques Verscheure, LTK 1957-65, vol. 6, col. 74.

13. Algermissen, *art. cit.* col. 907.

14. Algermissen, *ibid.* For the reception of Catholic Action in the dioceses of Germany in the years from 1928 to 1938 see the thorough investigation by Angelika Steinmaus-Pollak (*Das als Katholische Aktion organisierte Laienapostolat*, Würzburg 1988). She defines Catholic Action in Germany in this decade as "the form of the organized lay apostolate that was established or commissioned more or less explicitly as such by the competent Church authority" (p. 447).

15. In this mobilization of the laity were not similar aims displayed as were to be found in the ideological programmes of the various fascist systems establishing themselves at this time: uniformity in place of freedom of opinion, hierarchical control and centralism in place of democratic co-determination, and separation of powers?

Binding the laity more closely to the hierarchy did not of course exclude fierce confrontations in practice between lay associations and the hierarchy. In Switzerland, for example, the demand of the Catholic women's movement for political equality did not spark off any unanimous enthusiasm among the hierarchy (cf. on this subject U. Altermatt, *Katholizismus und Moderne*, Zürich 1989, pp. 209-16).

rection that was urgently needed but at the same time find itself
brought to an end.[16]

Pius XII distanced himself from the concept of hierarchical
apostolate. Rather he declared that the apostolate that was meant
remained always the apostolate of the laity and did not even become the hierarchical apostolate when it was exercised at the behest of the hierarchy.[17] In this Pius XII quite clearly contradicted
his predecessor. He was thus the first pope to see the Church
embodied in the laity. To put it succinctly, while for Pius XI the
laity essentially belong to the Church, for Pius XII they are the
Church. In 1946 he stated: "The faithful, and more precisely
the laity, stand in the foremost line of the Church's life. For them
the Church is the vital principle of human society. Hence they,
especially they, should have an ever clearer awareness not just
of belonging to the Church but of being the Church."[18] What is
obviously expressed in this contradiction of his predecessor by
one pope is a genuine symptom of crisis in the traditional model
of the Church. Typically, as we shall see, Vatican II drew back
from this insight.

Meanwhile in 1953 the French Dominican Yves Congar presented, in 683 pages, the first broadly-based attempt at a theology of the laity.[19] On the one hand Congar prepared the way for
Vatican II's vision of the Church as the people of God. On the
other hand the idea of the Church as the mystical body of Christ

---

16. It was granted some kind of survival by Vatican II, which again reverted
to the concept of Catholic Action (see below).

17. Verscheure, *art. cit.* col. 75.

18. Address to newly created cardinals, 20 February 1946, *Acta Apostolicae
Sedis* (AAS) 38 (1946), p. 149. Elmar Klinger (in Klinger and Rolf Zerfass [ed.],
Die Kirche der Laien. Eine Weichenstellung des Konzils, Würzburg 1987, p. 74)
also refers to the closing document of the Latin American Bishops' Conference at Puebla in 1979: "Young people must feel that they are the Church
through experiencing the Church as a place of community and co-operation."
Cf. also *Herder-Korrespondenz* 33 (1979), p. 524.

19. *Jalons pour une théologie du laïcat*, Paris 1953, ²1964; English translation
Lay People in the Church: A Study for a Theology of Laity, London/Dublin
1965. Yves Congar, born 1904, joined the Dominicans in 1926, had his licence
to teach theology in the name of the Church withdrawn and was banished from
Paris in 1954, a *peritus* at Vatican II in 1962, made a cardinal in 1994, died
1995.

was decisive for him in the wake of Pius XII's 1943 encyclical *Mystici Corporis Christi*. This surprisingly led Congar, contrary to the Pauline metaphor in the context of 1 Corinthians 12, to a morphological division of the Church into hierarchy and laity. Only the hierarchical functions guaranteed the Church its structure as an institution of salvation, and in this sense it is only the hierarchy that is essential for the existence of the Church.

However, for the Church to be able to fulfil its mission in the world it needs the laity. They belong integrally to the body of Christ, which can only completely develop its life in its totality, above all because the laity have access to areas of the world that remain closed to the hierarchy. "The faithful are the *pleroma* of the hierarchy," said Congar.[20] Even Congar could basically sooner conceive a Church without laity than without hierarchy. In this he was a child of his time. Anyone who has experienced this himself or herself will readily admit that he behaved more hierarchically than he understood himself to be.

So we should not be surprised if the Council's statements on this subject were disappointing.

2: The Second Vatican Council

Talk of the discovery of the laity in the twentieth century refers above all to the Second Vatican Council. This pretty well counts as the laity's *Magna Carta*. But when we look more closely we are grossly disappointed. What the Council had to say about the laity is expressed above all in three of its documents: the decree on the lay apostolate, *Apostolicam Actuositatem*; the decree on the Church's missionary activity, *Ad Gentes*; and the dogmatic constitution on the Church, *Lumen Gentium*. At least two of these need to be examined a little more closely.

The decree on the apostolate of laypeople, adopted on 18 November 1965, is not a fundamental statement about the position of the laity in the Church. Rather this document—which is rather wordy and resembles a bishop's Lenten pastoral rather than a declaration on behalf of the universal Church—is concerned, as its title indicates, to indicate to the laity their task in

---

20. *Op. cit.* (English), p. 455.

the Church's apostolate. By apostolate, as the decree spells out
somewhat laboriously, is understood every activity of the mystical body that serves the aim of bringing the whole world into
the right relationship with Christ (§ 2). The role accorded to
the laity in this arises from what they are, what they should do,
and what they can do in the Church.

The laity are of course involved in two domains, the spiritual
and the temporal (§ 5). Nevertheless the Council sees their duty
as lying principally in representing Jesus' cause in the world.
They thus become a link between the hierarchical Church, which
has no access to the world, and everyday life. The Church's pastors have the task of expounding the principles governing the
purpose of creation and the use to be made of the world and to
develop and proclaim guidelines, while the laity have the task of
acting in the world, guided by the "mind of the Church" (§ 6-
7). This and similar terminology repeatedly suggests that the
laity may belong to the Church but are only the Church in a
qualified and limited sense. They "have an active part of their
own in the life and action of the Church," and without their
action "the apostolate of the pastors will frequently be unable
to obtain its full effect." Particularly through catechetical instruction they "ardently co-operate in the spread of the Word of
God," but they are not independent (§ 10).

Surprisingly the Council goes on to raise the concept of Catholic Action—a somewhat woolly term in its definition—to new
heights. Among the "institutions" in which for several decades
"laypeople . . . formed themselves into various kinds of movements and societies" it singles out for special mention Catholic
Action, which is described as "a collaboration of the laity in the
hierarchical apostolate" (*cooperatio laicorum in apostolatu
hierarchico*; § 20). In his commentary on this passage F.
Klostermann remarks: "The laity is here still conceived of too
much in the sense of a body which exists for the execution of
tasks, as 'an extended arm of the hierarchy'. . . . Such a definition does not do justice to . . . the genuine co-responsibility of
the laity within the Church."[21]

21. H. Vorgrimler (ed.), *Commentary on the Documents of Vatican II*, London and New York 1967-9, vol. 3, p. 355.

The document's effort to make the laity properly subordinate to the hierarchy—something forced on it by interventions by Council Fathers—is often visible. Laypeople may have the right to form and run associations, but only "while preserving intact the necessary link with ecclesiastical authority" (§ 19). No apostolic organization formed by the laity "must lay claim to the name 'Catholic' if it has not the approval of legitimate ecclesiastical authority" (§ 24). That means the bishops decide who and what may call itself Catholic. Hence for example a group of workers cannot form itself into a "Catholic Workers' Movement" without this title receiving the bishops' blessing, however much emphasis is placed on the laity's "rightful freedom to act on their own initiative" (§ 24).

To sum up: the laity are an indispensable tool in the Church's apostolic activity but they are subordinate to the hierarchical officials responsible for this.

The classic expression of the Council's views on the laity and their relationship to the hierarchy is, however, to be found in the dogmatic constitution on the Church, *Lumen Gentium*. The constitution's outstanding statements are to be found in the second chapter, "The People of God" (*De populo Dei*). According to this Jesus instituted a new covenant and thereby "called a race made up of Jews and Gentiles which would be one, not according to the flesh, but in the Spirit, and this race would be the new People of God" (§ 9). The Church, in the sense of Congar's vision of it, is thus defined as the people of God and any and every class distinction within it is fundamentally rejected.[22] "Not only were the officials—pope, bishops, and clergy—now numbered among the 'people of God' but as the people of God all the Church's members, in advance of and without regard to all

22. The commentators point to the shift in meaning of the term "people of God" that took place in the course of the Council debates. "Whereas to begin with, after the successful treatment of office and ministry in the Church, it was to have been given precedence over the other individual categories of non-ministerial members of the Church as a collective concept, it was finally given precedence over all subsequent differentiations between officials, religious, laity, etc. along with the biblical idea of the 'Church as mystery'" (Dietrich Wiederkehr, "'Volk Gottes' erster und zweiter Klasse?" in *"Wir sind Kirche"— Das Kirchenvolksbegehren in der Diskussion*, Freiburg-im-Breisgau 1995, p. 113).

further subsequent differentiation, now obtained a common dignity and a common status as free agents. . . . It is neither a case of the members of the 'people of God' being added on to the officials from outside, nor are the officials contrasted with the laity of the 'people of God' as if they were on different platforms, but in advance of any differentiation and subsuming this they form together (and only together) the 'people of God'."[23]

This new people of God is further consecrated as a holy priesthood, which is, however, essentially distinct from the hierarchical priesthood (§ 10).[24] "Each disciple of Christ has the obligation of spreading the faith to the best of his ability." Hence each is competent to administer baptism. But it is of course reserved to the priest to "complete the building up of the body in the eucharistic sacrifice" (§ 17).

This provides the transition to the third chapter on the hierarchical constitution of the Church (§§ 18-29). It is difficult to think of a greater contrast than that between chapter 2 of the dogmatic constitution on the one hand and chapters 3 and 4 on the other. What is given with one hand is here taken away by the other. Dietrich Wiederkehr talks of an "extensive lack of connection between the fundamental second chapter on the people of God and the third chapter that follows immediately and suddenly on the hierarchy, the papal primacy and the college of bishops."[25]

This chapter moreover occupies roughly twice as much space as the succeeding chapter on the laity. First of all it reaffirms

---

23. Wiederkehr, *op. cit.*, pp. 113-4.

24. With this the Council endorsed an existing state of affairs. Even those who at that time advocated the universal priesthood of the faithful in Council circles did not have the remotest idea of calling into question the conventional division of the priestly dignity, cf. B. E. J. de Smedt (bishop of Bruges), *Vom allgemeinen Priestertum der Gläubigen*, Munich 1962. The fact that the distinction between the ministerial and universal priesthood is already taken up here is displeasing and must be connected with the constitution's progress through the Council and the tensions this aroused (see note 22 above).

25. Dietrich Wiederkehr, "Sensus vor Consensus: auf dem Weg zu einem partizipativen Glauben—Reflexionen einer Wahrheitspolitik," in Wiederkehr (ed.), Der *Glaubenssinn des Gottesvolkes—Konkurrent oder Partner des Lehramts?*, Freiburg-im-Breisgau 1994, p. 182. On the consequences that should have resulted from the concept of the "people of God" for the Church's structures

the divine prerogatives (privileges/distinctions) that the First
Vatican Council had ascribed to the Bishop of Rome—primacy
and infallibility (§ 18, cf. §§ 22, 25). By the will of Jesus the other
bishops are meant as successors of the apostles to govern as pastors "until the end of the world" (§ 18). The office of bishop
thus depends on divine institution. At the same time the saying
Jesus directed to his disciples—"He who hears you hears me"
(Luke 10:16)—is restricted to the bishops (§ 20). In them Jesus
Christ, the high priest, is present among the faithful. Through
their wisdom and prudence he guides the people of God of the
New Covenant to eternal blessedness. They possess the pleni-
tude of the sacrament of order and thus the high priesthood (§
21, cf. § 28).

After the long-winded and ponderous statements about bishops the constitution is relatively brief when it comes to priests
and deacons. Priests may not enjoy the highest degree of priestly
orders, but are nevertheless linked with the bishops in the priestly
dignity. It is principally in the celebration of the eucharist that
they exercise their office (§ 28). Deacons, finally, are one degree
lower in the hierarchy. They receive the laying on of hands "not
unto the priesthood, but unto the ministry" of service (§ 29).

In the fourth chapter the Council finally turns its attention to
"the state of those Christians who are called the laity." In this
way they are seen as a separate class ("*status*"), however this term
should be understood. Together with religious and clergy they
form the people of God. Since the "ordained pastors" are not
in a position "to undertake alone the whole salvific mission of
the Church to the world" they need the single-minded co-operation of the laity (§ 30). The latter thus emerge as assistants to
the hierarchy. They are distinguished from the clergy by their
secular or temporal character. Although "those in holy orders
may sometimes be engaged in secular activities, or even practice

and institutions but were not able to, owing to the solidly embedded doctrinal
formulations and structural organization, see further Wiederkehr, "Ekklesiologie
und Kirchen-Innenpolitik. Protokoll eines Re-lecture des Kirchenkonstitution
von Vaticanum II," in M. Kessler and others (ed.), *Fides quaerens intellectum.
Festschrift für Max Seckler*, Tübingen 1992: "The harsh monopoly of the clergy
is no longer to be evaded with the weak images of the people of God" (p. 257).

a secular profession," it is nevertheless the business of the laity "to seek the kingdom of God by engaging in temporal affairs and directing them according to God's will" (§ 31). Although "the Lord" (*sic*) may have made a distinction between "the sacred ministers and the rest of the people of God," nevertheless both "are joined together by a close relationship" (§ 32). And although an apostolate is already incumbent upon the laity in the Church thanks to baptism and confirmation, they can also be "called in different ways to more immediate co-operation in the apostolate of the hierarchy" (§ 33).

Since Christ, the eternal high priest, wishes to continue his ministry through the laity "also," he "also" gives them a share in his priestly office (§ 34). Similarly he fulfils his prophetic office "not only by the hierarchy . . ., but also by the laity." Furthermore, "when there are no sacred ministers or when these are impeded under persecution, some lay people supply sacred functions to the best of their ability" (§ 35).

Thanks to their competence in secular disciplines the laity have a special place in the sanctification of the world. They should unite harmoniously their rights and duties in the Church and in society (§ 36). The laity have above all the right to receive in abundance from their pastors the help of the word of God and of the sacraments. In return they should promptly accept (*amplectantur*) what is decided by their pastors as representatives of Christ. The latter for their part should make use of the laity's advice, grant them freedom of action, and attentively consider their suggestions and wishes (§ 37).

This document has been interpreted in a variety of ways and to a great extent positively. Above all it provides the basis for what has become the generally accepted view that the Council gained a quite new vision of the laity and inaugurated the era of the laity.[26] Now it was no longer a question of clergy and laity

---

26. "The Council comprehensively determined the position of the laity in the Church" (Klinger and Zerfass [ed.], *Die Kirche der Laien*, p. 15). "There is no doubt that with regard to the identity and position of the laity in the Church the Second Vatican Council brought about a fundamental transformation" (Kurt Koch, *Kirche der Laien? Plaidoyer für die göttliche Würde der Laien in der Kirche*, Fribourg 1991, p. 11).

being opposed to each other as superior and subordinate, the hierarchy as the Church and the laity as the people; rather they both together formed the people of God. "The hierarchy is people, and the laity are also Church."[27] In this context reference was made to Pius XII's 1946 statement, according to which the laity could say of themselves: "We do not only belong to the Church—we are the Church."[28] But this is precisely what the Council did not say. Admittedly, with the customary reference to 1 Peter 2:4–10, it brought out the "universal priesthood" of all believers.[29] It also made it clear that the office of the laity is not a share in the hierarchical office of the clergy but in the priestly, prophetic, and kingly office of Christ. This however does not in any way alter the fact that for the Council the ministerial priesthood and the universal priesthood differ in essence. And in this way the Council underwrote yet again the fatal two-tier structure of the Church. The equality of all members of the Church asserted by the Council refers merely to the "common dignity" of all believers (§ 32). This is hardly designed "to close the gap that has grown up over centuries between 'priests' and 'laypeople'."[30]

What above all is missing from the Council's documents is a clear definition of the laity. According to the decree on the Church's missionary activity, *Ad Gentes*, the laity are "Christians who have been incorporated into Christ through baptism and live in the world" (§ 15). But since all the faithful, whether clerical or lay, have logically been "incorporated into Christ," what is special about the laity is clearly their living in the world. In the decree on the apostolate of the laity this aspect is expounded somewhat more broadly. According to this document the characteristic of the lay state is "a life led in the midst of the world and of secular affairs." Hence the laity "are called by God to make of their apostolate, through the vigour of their Chris-

27. Klinger and Zerfass, *op. cit.* p. 71.

28. *Ibid.*, p. 73.

29. For the dubious nature of talk of the "universal priesthood" see the excursus on this subject, pp. 69–72 below.

30. Alexsander Rajšp, *"Priester" und "Laien." Ein neues Verständnis*. Düsseldorf 1982, p. 100.

tian spirit, a leaven in the world" (*Apostolicam Actuositatem* § 2).
The dogmatic constitution on the Church, *Lumen Gentium*,
served as a model for this decree.

The secular character—*indoles saecularis*—of the laity underlined by the Council is dealt with in a variety of ways. There
was no lack of voices to warn the Council not to imply it was
allotting the sphere of the Church to the hierarchy and the sphere
of the world to the laity. "As if through the back door the division between laity and clergy was re-introduced in the reception of Vatican II through too sharp a distinction between Church
and world, according to which the service of the world belonged
to the laity but on the other hand the service of salvation in the
Church belonged to the clergy. With this the laity were firmly
placed in the sphere outside the Church. In contrast to this tendency the Council itself emphasized . . . that laypeople have their
place in both Church and world and enjoy their rights in both."[31]

Nevertheless, do not the Council documents themselves suggest the interpretation that is here rejected? And above all has
not this interpretation become the dominant practice since the
Council? Within the Church the hierarchy have a free hand to
run things autonomously (for example, the appointment of bishops), while the laity do not have a say and are relegated to secular affairs. But even here they cannot enjoy their freedom. This
is limited by the hierarchy in matters of marriage, the family,
society, and politics, and disappears completely where sexuality
is involved.[32]

In order to make up the continuing deficiency in the laity's
position the Council frequently referred to the laity's participation in Christ's priestly, prophetic, and kingly office as its par-

---

31. Neuner, *Der Laie und das Gottesvolk* (note 1 above), p. 129; cf. also
Elisabeth Braunbeck, *Der Weltcharakter des Laien. Eine theologisch-rechtliche
Untersuchung im Licht des II. Vatikanischen Konzils*, Regensburg 1993, p. 141.

32. Leo Karrer, *Aufbruch der Christen. Das Ende der klerikalen Kirchen*, Munich 1989, pp. 83-4: "At work in the background in the relevant official documents is a secret dualism, a contradiction, which has its effect on the role allotted to the laity. On the one hand they are sent out into the world (*missio*)
while on the other within the Church with its present structure they are fenced
off (*communio*). . . . This, however, is fundamentally the old pattern of the patriarchal separation of clergy and laity."

ticular distinguishing mark. This is already present in the opening declaration of *Lumen Gentium*.

But when it comes to describing this participation in Christ's threefold office in greater detail, things become problematic. Through the stereotypes of the language of ecclesiastical spirituality the tendency to spiritualize this theological concept becomes tangible: its sense and meaning evaporate completely when applied in practice.

According to the dogmatic constitution on the Church Jesus gives the laity "a share in his priestly office, to offer spiritual worship." "Anointed with the Holy Spirit," they can offer "spiritual sacrifices" through their prayer, their apostolic undertakings, their family and married life, their daily work, their patient endurance of the hardships of life (*Lumen Gentium* § 34). In unctuous language things that should be taken for granted are not only proclaimed a spiritual category but also linked with a hypocritical mystique of suffering, the effects of which penetrate as far as the celebration of the eucharist.

Similarly Jesus fulfils his "prophetic office, not only by the hierarchy . . ., but also by the laity." They become "powerful heralds of the faith in things to be hoped for if they join unhesitating profession of faith to the life of faith," which means "proclaiming the gospel through word and deed and in this way co-operating in building up the kingdom of Christ in the world" (§ 35). It seems to me questionable whether this really pins down what is essential in the prophetic office. There does not seem to be here any thought of criticism of or resistance to the established political and religious system, a characteristic of Israelite prophecy; nor of the idea that a prophet is an interpreter of God (and not necessarily automatically of the Church). And the restriction demanded of the laity by the new code of canon law when it comes to preaching the word will be shown in the following chapter.[33]

Finally, should it not also belong to the prophetic office, and in fact specially so, that the faithful—as the Council itself teaches

---

33. As far as Weis is concerned, the prophetic office of the laity in practice coincides in its actual exercise with the lay apostolate.

(*Dei Verbum* § 8)—contribute to progress in understanding the tradition of faith? From this point of view the concept of the Church's teaching authority would need to be given a completely new definition, since the laity too would be included in those exercising it instead of being merely the object of its attention. But here too practice lags behind theory, as Dietrich Wiederkehr has clearly diagnosed: "Among the people of God too many have so far never yet had the possibility of taking part in the discovery of truth and thus merely exercising the dignity of active agents. The reverse of this is that so far the teaching authority has never yet seen itself faced with the demand of letting its existing monopoly be broken up and allowing the whole of the rest of the people of God to share in the common responsibility for the truth..... It is not enough if the existing teaching authority benevolently welcomes and encourages the awakening of the sense of faith among the faithful and in congregations without understanding itself in a new and different way within this collective agent. . . . In this way the teaching authority is still living an extraterritorial existence immune to analysis."[34]

What finally does the laity's participation in Christ's kingdom consist of? According to the dogmatic constitution on the Church Jesus' disciples, "by self-abnegation and a holy life, overcome the reign of sin in themselves . . . [and] bring their brethren to that king to serve whom is to reign" (§ 36). This means nothing other than that everyone who serves God (= king) also shares in his reign. The Council does not seem to envisage codetermination with regard to the kingly laity. Furthermore, it cannot be overlooked that in the entire dogmatic constitution on the Church the laity ultimately appear instrumentalized as assistants of the hierarchy. They remain the object of hierarchical power, without ever being able to be the agent of autonomous action as Church. As has been shown above, the Council draws a sharp dividing line between the "ordained pastors" and the laity, whose universal priesthood differs in essence from the hierarchical priesthood (§ 10).

The distinction between *clerus* and *plebs*, the differentiation

---

34. Wiederkehr, *Sensus vor Consensus* (note 25 above), pp. 191 and 198.

of the laity from the "ordained pastors," runs like a scarlet thread
through the entire constitution on the Church. Thus it is striking how often the Council documents use the word "also" when
they are talking about the laity. The way should be clear for the
laity *also* to share diligently in the salvific work of the Church (§
33). It is through the laity *also* that Jesus Christ wishes to continue his witness and his service, and so he *also* gives them a
share in his priestly office (§ 34). It is *also* by the laity that he
fulfils his prophetic office (§ 35), and he desires his kingdom to
be spread *also* "by the lay faithful" (§ 36). What sounds like an
addition is in fact a limitation. First come the priests, then the
laity follow. If the laity have the right and indeed the duty to
express their opinion, nevertheless they "should promptly accept in Christian obedience what is decided by the pastors who,
as teachers and rulers of the Church, represent Christ" (§ 37).

What above all is surprising is the omission of the gospel statements on discipleship and following Christ. To define the laity
the Council Fathers (and their theologians) did not need the gospel. In the whole of the chapter on the laity in the dogmatic constitution on the Church there are only two references to the gospels: one to Matthew 20:28 (Jesus came not to be served but to
serve) (§ 32), and one to Matthew 5:3-9 (the beatitudes blessing
the poor, the meek, the peacemakers) (§ 38). If the Council had
let itself be guided by the gospel of discipleship and following
Christ, it would have dealt infinitely more easily with the "ordained pastors" and the laity.[35]

3: The new code of canon law

One result of the Council was the reform of canon law. This
was announced along with the Council by Pope John XXIII on
25 January 1959 in the chapter-house of St Paul's without the
Walls. "As a result the Council and the reform of canon law are
from the start closely linked to each other."[36] The revised code

35. As a model for this a book that might serve is K. H. Schelkle, *Jüngerschaft
und Apostelamt*, Freiburg-im-Breisgau 1957, English translation *Discipleship and
Priesthood*, London 1966.

36. Richard Puza, "Der Laie im neuen Codex Juris Canonici," in *Theologische
Quartalschrift* 164 (1984), pp. 88-102, here p. 88.

of canon law published in 1983 was intended by the will of the Pope to bear the stamp of the Council. Consequently the prescriptions about the "obligations and rights of the lay members of Christ's faithful" (canons 224–31) closely follow the fourth chapter of *Lumen Gentium*.[37]

The new code does admittedly fix things in advance by confirming the existence of two classes in the Church—and indeed, in contradiction to the historical evidence, deriving this from a divine instruction. "By divine institution [*ex divina institutione*], among Christ's faithful there are in the Church sacred ministers, who in law are also called clerics; the others are called lay people" (canon 207 § 1). Once again the laity are the non-clerics, the others. Hence it is no wonder that even in the code of canon law it is difficult to find a positive definition of the laity.

According to canon 225 the layperson is that member of Christ's faithful who is incorporated into the people of God through the sacrament of baptism and, perfected by the sacrament of confirmation, shares in the Church's duty of proclaiming salvation. In particular, as in the Council documents, he or she must order temporal affairs in the spirit of the gospel.[38] Here too the duties of the laity that are singled out for mention deal with matters that could be taken for granted. If they are married, they have "the special obligation . . . to strive for the building up of the people of God through their marriage and family" and "to ensure the Christian education of their children in accordance with the teaching of the Church" (canon 226).

Rights and duties are indeed mentioned alternately. However the duties are naturally derived from the rights. Thus from the fundamental right and the fundamental duty of sharing in the Church's mission of salvation (canon 225) arises also the right

---

37. On this subject see Puza, *Katholisches Kirchenrecht*, Heidelberg 1986, and also his article cited in the preceding note; also Peter Boekholt, *Der Laie in der Kirche. Seine Rechte und Pflichten im neuen Kirchenrecht*, Kevelaer 1984; Gustave Thils, *Les Laïcs dans le nouveau Code de Droit Canonique et au IIe Concile du Vatican*, Louvain-la-Neuve 1983.

38. Cf. Puza, *art. cit.*, pp. 90–1. Puza notes that in canon 225 participation in the Church's mission is mentioned before service in the world. But the question of course is where the laity are to fulfil the Church's duty of proclaiming salvation if not in the world.

of laypeople to study theology and to receive "from the lawful ecclesiastical authority" a mandate to teach theology (canon 229).

In the liturgical field presiding at the celebration of the eucharist remains a privilege of the clergy. "The only minister who, in the person of Christ, can bring into being the sacrament of the eucharist is a validly ordained priest" (canon 900 §1). Laymen can be permanently commissioned in the office of reader or acolyte; laywomen can merely be assigned the role of reader temporarily. Additional possibilities only arise when there is a lack of ordained ministers or liturgically commissioned readers or acolytes (canon 230).[39]

The most restrictive prescriptions of the new code of canon law concern the proclamation of the word of God. Even if the absolute ban on lay preaching found in the 1917 code (canon 1342 § 2) is not maintained, preaching by laypeople in a church remains restricted to exceptional cases and within the eucharist it is entirely reserved to the priest or deacon (canons 766 and 767).[40] Efforts by the German bishops' conference in Rome to have lay preaching allowed at Mass remained unsuccessful.[41] This clearly shows the limits set to the unceasingly invoked participation of the laity in Christ's prophetic office.[42]

The same applies to the office of leadership. "Those who are in sacred orders are . . . capable of the power of governance," even if laypeople "can co-operate [*cooperari possunt*] in the exercise of this same power" (canon 129, cf. canon 228).[43]

---

39. *Ibid.*, pp. 95-6.

40. *Ibid.*, p. 96.

41. Adrian Loretan, *Laien im pastoralen Dienst*, Fribourg 1994, pp. 120-5.

42. The conclusion of Carlos J. Errázuriz (*"Munus docendi Ecclesiae." Diritti e doveri dei fedeli*, Milan 1991) is that the faithful have both the right and the duty to receive the word of God and to preserve and deepen it in subjection to the magisterium. The proclamation of the word of God, however, is not something that belongs to them on the ground of their status but only in their capacity as collaborators with officials of the hierarchy.

43. According to Werner Böckenförde "the old understanding of the Church as a *societas inaequalis* [unequal society] dominates in current canon law." He underlines this judgment with a quotation from the address that Pope Paul VI gave toward the end of the Council to the commission he had formed for the reform of canon law: "Laypeople lack the capability of leadership. They are subordinated to the hierarchy and bound in conscience to obey the laws in keep-

What this co-operation consists of is not stated.[44] The commentators meanwhile emphasize that as far as the rights and duties of the laity according to the code of canon law are concerned we need to consider not only those prescriptions that concern the laity exclusively but also those dealing with all Christ's faithful, to whom ultimately both clergy and laity belong. According to the canon lawyer Richard Puza,[45] there are in all eighteen rights belonging to all the faithful. Among these is "the right to public opinion. Christians are free to express their opinion on matters that concern the Church not only to the Church authorities but also to other members of the Church. The code thus opens up a respectable space for the development of public opinion in the Church."

Nevertheless, anyone examining the new 1983 code of canon law on the subject of the laity will steer clear of the idea that with the twentieth century the age of the laity has been rung in, even if in individual countries the letter of the law has been overtaken by practice in certain fields (e.g. women readers, lay preaching). Instead of carrying the work of the Council forward the code is already twenty years behind its stipulations.[46] As far as the new code is concerned the Catholic Church is and remains a clerical Church.[47]

---

ing with the saying: 'He who hears you hears me, and he who rejects you rejects me' (Luke 10:16). The new code of canon law was drawn up in keeping with this papal statement" ("Statement aus der Sicht eines Kirchenrechtlers" in Wiederkehr (ed.), *Der Glaubenssinn des Gottesvolkes*, pp. 207-13, this reference p. 208).

44. Puza, *Katholisches Kirchenrecht*, Heidelberg 1986, p. 134, has judges in church courts in mind.

45. Puza, *art. cit.*, p. 94.

46. Puza, *op. cit.*, pp. 134, 161-2.

47. When Boekholt (note 37) praises the new code for finally doing away with the disastrous view that in the Church there are two mutually exclusive groups, clergy and laity (p. 9), one can only murmur that unfortunately this is not the case.

4: The 1987 synod

The subject of the seventh ordinary synod of bishops, which met in Rome from 1 to 30 October 1987, was "The vocation and mission of the laity in the Church and in the world twenty years after the Second Vatican Council." It is the latest solemn indication by the entire official Church of its views on the role played by laypeople in the Church. The wording indicates a taking stock of the effects the Council's decisions had brought about. On this Pope John Paul II wrote in his post-synodal document *Christifideles Laici* (see below) of the Fathers "following the path marked out by the Council" (§ 2). The challenge they embraced was in reality "that of indicating the concrete ways through which this rich 'theory' on the lay state expressed by the Council can be translated into authentic Church 'practice'" (§ 2).[48]

So there was originally reason to hope that the synod would make good the deficiencies of the Council's pronouncements on the laity by adopting broader perspectives. But already the 1985 *Lineamenta*, the outline preparatory document for the synod, gave rise to fears that this hope would be disappointed.[49] Of the one hundred and forty-two people to whom the *Lineamenta* were sent eighty answered with responses that were evaluated in 1987 in an *Instrumentum laboris*, which also gave rise to serious concern.[50] Even if subsequently about sixty laypeople were invited to the synod as auditors,[51] it was nevertheless an explicitly episcopal synod in which the bishops were to pronounce on the life and mission of the laity.

---

48. For details of the synod see *Synode des Evêques. Les Laïcs dans l'Eglise et dans le monde*, Paris 1987.

49. "The *Lineamenta* do not in any case provide a convincing prelude for the synod on the laity. Without exception the document lacks contact with reality" (U. Ruh, *Herder-Korrespondenz* 39 [1985], p. 157).

50. According to U. Ruh (*Herder-Korrespondenz* 41 [1987], p. 258) "the text ignores . . . precisely the decisive problems." What particularly caused offence was the sentence: "The mission proper to ordained ministers is to proclaim the faith in the world with full doctrinal authority; the laity on the other hand have the mission of bearing witness to the faith."

51. In his opening address the Pope described the laypeople present as "necessarily few in number."

In other words, it was the hierarchy that discussed and determined what the laity are for and what their task is in Church and world. The two classes, clergy and laity, were not analyzed but declared to complement each other.[52] But it was in the person of the bishop that the Church preferentially took shape, as the Pope stated in his opening address on 1 October.

On the position of women "unexpected advances . . . were not undertaken. The possibility of the ordination of women was not on the agenda, and only a handful pleaded for women to be admitted to the diaconate."[53] To the regret of Catholic public opinion the synod closed without issuing a final document.[54] All it did was to draw up fifty-four propositions for the Pope to use as raw material for an apostolic exhortation he was asked to write to conclude the synod's work. These gave critical observers the impression of a "withered skeleton," indeed in places of a "mixed grocery stall."[55] All the same it is surprising to read: "It is in the parish that the major part of Catholics learn that they, gathered together in the communion of saints, are the Church or a part of the Church." One has the impression of hearing Pius XII in 1946 (see p. 16 above).

The post-synodal apostolic exhortation which the synod fathers asked the Pope to write takes its title from its opening words, *Christifideles laici*, and bears the date of 30 December 1988 (though actually published at noon on 30 January 1989). It is the most comprehensive post-synodal document to have appeared so far. According to the document's introductory remarks the laity belong to that people of God denoted in the parable of

---

52. "There was no desire to give up . . . the class division into laity, clergy, and religious, although developments within the Church are already leading to new interactions becoming apparent" (*Herder-Korrespondenz* 41 [1987], p. 523).

53. *Ibid*. p. 525. Ludwig Kaufmann also mentioned the "suppressed question of women" in his reports in *Orientierung* 51 (1987), pp. 191-4 and 225-7.

54. The reports in leading daily newspapers evinced an understandable frustration, for example: "The Catholic bishops' synod has problems about giving the laity further powers" (*Süddeutsche Zeitung*, 17 October 1987); "No new initiatives from the synod of bishops" (*Neue Zürcher Zeitung*, 31 October/1 November 1987).

55. *Herder-Korrespondenz*, 41 (1987) pp. 564-5.

the labourers in the vineyard (Matt. 20:1-16). Admittedly a little later (§ 9) Pius XII's famous saying whereby the laity do not merely belong to the Church but are the Church is quoted (see p. 16 above). For the rest the document depends considerably on Vatican II, with a remarkable number of direct quotations from that council's documents:[56] baptism as the basis for the dignity and mission of the laity; sharing in Christ's priestly, prophetic and kingly office; the secular character of the laity; their vocation to holiness; the Church as communion.

The "ordained ministries" derive from the sacrament of orders and are "a grace for the entire Church," even if the ministerial priesthood "essentially has the royal priesthood of all the faithful as its aim and is ordered to it" (§ 22). The desire for a liturgical empowerment of the laity that would go beyond the Council and the new code of canon law is met by the setting-up of an appropriate commission. The statements about women appear remarkable. Although Jesus did not call women, in distinction to men, "to the apostolate of the Twelve and thereby to the ministerial priesthood" (§ 49), women nevertheless, like men, share in Christ's threefold office. Two great tasks are particularly entrusted to women: "bringing full dignity to the conjugal life and to motherhood" and "assuring the moral dimension of culture" (§ 51).

To sum it all up: from Vatican II through the 1983 code of canon law to *Christifideles laici* nothing has moved in the Catholic Church as far as concerns the evaluation of the laity.[57]

5: The debate continues

The fact that the discussion of the laity at Vatican II and the 1987 synod of bishops was not very productive nevertheless had the benefit that the debate continued more strongly. It is quite obvious that, despite all the efforts to disguise things, the gap between hierarchy and laity continues to exist and is experienced

---

56. Ninety-seven of the total of 224 footnotes refer to documents of Vatican II (*Herder-Korrespondenz* 43 [1989], p. 106).

57. Beyond this, for example, the president of the pontifical council for the laity is a cardinal or archbishop.

as something that causes suffering. Reminders have been campaigns by laypeople such as the Church referendum—*Kirchenvolksbegehren*—launched in Austria and Germany and the reactions of the bishops to it.

Indignation at the patronizing of those who understand themselves to be Church but are not taken seriously as such despite all the fine words about the "hour of the laity" is expressed in strong words from individual theologians but especially from disappointed and despairing laypeople. According to Dietrich Wiederkehr, "those in positions of leadership in the Church continually betray how they still see themselves in a possible, freely eligible, independent state of autonomy from which they, perhaps graciously and condescendingly, can open themselves to the concerns of the faithful, or perhaps not. . . . It shows how far removed from the people of God and split off from them are those who bear office when they think they are still able to consider whether they wish to be affected at all by a demand from the community."[58]

Werner Holzgreve writes on Vatican II's dogmatic constitution on the Church, *Lumen Gentium*: "In the context of the entire constitution of the Church many passages of *Lumen Gentium* have not remained free from contradictions and reservations. Many passages once again relativize progressive statements about the Church—or on closer examination cut them right back. There is no doubt that greater weight is attributed to the sacrament of orders and thus to the person who is ordained and particularly to the pastors than to the laity."[59] So it must regretfully be admitted that "many passages of *Lumen Gentium*, through their woolliness and vagueness, but also though their repeated emphasizing of the magisterium and of hierarchical order in the Church provide the polemical ammunition for those powers aimed at restoration that seek to re-establish the Church once again as a 'house of glory' in which a super-pious inerrant landlord decides the price and content of the leases."[60]

---

58. Wiederkehr, "Volk Gottes" (note 22 above), pp. 114-5.

59. Werner Holzgreve, *Die Stunde der Laien ist da! Das Ende der Leidensbereitschaft an der Kirche*, Constance 1992, p. 53.

60. *Ibid.*, p. 55.

The apostolic exhortation *Christifideles Laici* inevitably invites the same criticism as Vatican II. In this the term "rank and file" crops up: "For the Pope . . . the laity are certainly an extremely valuable and indeed indispensable part of the people of God, but forming the rank and file which may belong essentially to the Church but are and must remain merely a retinue. Naturally the laity (including women, of course) should and indeed must co-operate, join in providing advice and share in missionary activity. But there is only one thing they must not do: share in decision-making."[61]

All these defects that arouse so much complaint do indeed have their roots in the structure of the Catholic Church as it started taking shape in the third century and was endorsed in 1870 at the First Vatican Council, which bestowed divine qualities on the pope. It is hard to understand why it is only in isolated instances, if at all, that one hears a demand for a change to this structure, for a completely new constitution for the Church and in keeping with this for a new council.[62] People talk only about

---

61. *Ibid.*, p. 61. The question can also be put in this way: "The laity—stepchildren or priests, prophets and kings?" (Stefanie Spendel in Gerhard Grohs and Gernot Czell, *Kirche in der Welt—Kirche der Laien?*, Frankfurt-am-Main 1990, pp. 131-50).

62. Neuner (*Der Laie und das Gottesvolk*, pp. 217-20) laments "that the idea of the Church as the people of God has not yet become something that determines its structure. As in the past, all important decisions are made not by the people of God but by a handful of office-bearers within the community or on its behalf. As in the past, all decision-making power is reserved to the clergy, and they are free to decide whether and how they will include the laity in the process of reaching a decision and whom they will call on for advice. . . . In the course of the Church's history a variety of powers and competences have accrued to the ministry that are not in any way necessarily connected with it nor are so because of the Church's nature and the way it was established." Admittedly Neuner goes on to regard as indispensable "above all . . . the office bestowed by ordination." Pascal Thomas (*Ces chrétiens qu'on appelle laïcs*, Paris 1988, p. 10) recalls that the laity "in fact form very nearly the totality of the Christian people."

bridging the gap between clergy and laity, hardly ever of doing away with it.[63] People do not want to see that the fundamental evil of the Church is its two-class system. As long as this is not done away with, all "reforms"are merely bits of sticking-plaster that do nothing to cure the real disease.

An unprejudiced look at the Gospels will show how diametrically opposed to Jesus's intentions the present constitution of the Catholic Church is, and this is what we must now undertake.

---

63. Noteworthy is the subtitle of the book by Rémi Parent, *Une Eglise de baptisés*, Paris 1987: *Pour surmonter l'opposition clercs/laïcs* (Overcoming the opposition between clergy and laity).

Chapter II

Jesus did not want any Priests

1. The Church's image of the priest

Our contemporary image of the priest is determined by many influences. It is above all the outcome of papal and episcopal teaching which is then developed in specialist and more popular writings and carried forward by traditional and popular piety. Here we shall concentrate on the actual sources, restricting ourselves to the past hundred years.

With the exception of Benedict XV (1914–22), who was pope during the First World War and thus had more urgent matters requiring his attention,[1] over the past century no pope has omitted to issue an encyclical or equivalent document either on the priesthood or addressed to priests—an indication of how far the clergy were a particular concern of the Church's leadership. Some of these documents have a doctrinal tone, such as Pius XI's encyclical *Ad Catholici Sacerdotii* of 20 December 1935. Others have an ascetic or pastoral character, concerned with the priest's life-style. To this class belong, for example, Pius X's exhortation to the Catholic clergy of 4 August 1908 on the priest's self-sanctification, Pius XII's apostolic exhortation *Menti Nostrae* of 23 September 1950 on the priestly life and recruitment to the priesthood today, and John XXIII's encyclical *Sacerdotii Nostri Primordia* of 1 August 1959 on the Curé d'Ars as the model of priesthood.[2]

---

1. Nevertheless mention should be made of his encyclical *Humani Generis* of 15 June 1917 on the significance of preaching.

2. Also to be noted is the document of the 1971 synod of bishops on the priesthood. The traditional ideas are based on the Council documents and are not inquired into further. The community of Christians cannot fulfil its mission completely without a priestly ministerial office (§8:2). This differs in kind and not just in degree from the universal priesthood of the faithful (§12:5). "Only the priest can act in the person of Christ when it is a question of presiding . . . at the sacrificial meal and validly effectuating it" (§12:7).

A combination of doctrinal teaching and exhortation can be found in Paul VI's encyclical on priestly celibacy, *Sacerdotalis Caelibatus*, of 24 June 1967. It is of course reasonable to assume that fundamental statements about the priesthood also find their way into and influence exhortatory documents.

In all this the arguments used to justify and describe the priest-hood remain the same. From the same source arise also the corresponding wrong developments. The unshakeable fundamental starting point is that at the last supper Jesus instituted the priesthood of the new covenant and ordained the "apostles" as priests.[3] Hence Pius XI justifies the subject and date of his encyclical on the priesthood in the "holy year" of 1933 on the basis that it is the nineteenth centenary of the institution of the priesthood.[4] This connection is trotted out in each of the letters

---

Finally the *Directory on the Ministry and Life of Priests* issued in 1994 by the Roman Congregation for the Clergy must count as authoritative for our times.

To be mentioned among episcopal writings are the statement on the priestly ministry issued in 1970 by the bishops of the German-speaking world (according to the title page, but in the document itself we find it is merely "the German bishops" who are speaking) and the statement of the German bishops on the priestly ministry of 24 Sept. 1992. The latter has a practical and pastoral tone, asking: "Who are we as priests? How can the priestly life be lived today?"

The weightier 1970 document distances itself from equating the last supper with ordination to the priesthood and recognizes the complicated historical development of the Church's priesthood. Nevertheless it had a very mixed reception among biblical scholars. Karl Kertelge (*Gemeinde und Amt im Neuen Testament*, Munich 1972, pp. 21-6) described it as "a theological endeavour to be taken seriously," while Wilhelm Pesch ("Priestertum und Neues Testament", in Pesch and others, *Priestertum—Kirchliches Amt zwischen gestern und morgen*, Aschaffenburg 1971, pp. 12-18) pays tribute to some of the statement having been "envisioned and undertaken in an exemplary manner" (p. 12) while nevertheless criticizing the zealous "defence of existing institutions and traditional doctrines" (p. 14). "Throughout the statement remains blind to the present and future possibilities of development in the leadership of Christian congregations" (p. 14).

3. *Ad Catholici Sacerdotii* § 13 and elsewhere. It is only Luke 22:14 that talks of "apostles": otherwise in the gospel accounts of the Last Supper we read of disciples (Mark 14:12, 32; Matt. 14;17), of the "twelve" (Mark 14:17), of the "twelve disciples" (Matt. 14:20). But the distinction between the "twelve," the "apostles," and the "disciples" that is taken for granted by contemporary exegesis is irrelevant for papal documents. As far as they are concerned it can only have been the "apostles," whatever should be understood by that term.

4. *Ad Catholici Sacerdotii* § 6.

that Pope John Paul II writes to the priests of the world every
year on Maundy Thursday.[5]

The fact that nowhere in the New Testament is there mention
of the apostles having made use of the priestly power entrusted
to them does not seem to worry anyone. Even in the case of Paul
the only thing we are certain of is that he took part in the celebration of the "breaking of bread" (Acts 20:7). Whether he ever
presided at the eucharist remains open.[6]

The failure to distinguish between the "twelve," the disciples,

---

5. The most recent example is that for 1996, when we read that at the Last
Supper, "Christ revealed to the Apostles that it was their vocation to become
priests like him and in him. . . . By entrusting to the Apostles the memorial of
his sacrifice, Christ made them sharers in his priesthood. . . . From the Apostles, then, we have inherited the priestly ministry" (*Briefing*, 18 April 1996).

The first of these Maundy Thursday letters, of 8 Apr. 1979, a year after John
Paul II's accession, found an unusual positive as well as negative echo, not least
because of its reinforcement of the obligation of celibacy (cf. Georg Denzler
(ed.), *Priester für heute*, Munich 1980, who on pp. 197-217 prints the whole
text of this letter). The introductory adaptation of Augustine's saying, "For you
I am a bishop, with you I am a Christian," into "For you I am a bishop, with
you I am a priest" presents the priest from the start as the perfection of the
Christian. The idea that the sacramental priesthood differs not only in degree
but also in kind from the universal priesthood of the faithful is emphasized
four times in this brief document in order to mark the priest off suitably in
every case from the ordinary people of the Church. The sacramental priesthood is "hierarchical," which means "linked to the power to form and lead the
priestly people." The obligation of celibacy rests on "apostolic teaching." Over
the years interest in these Maundy Thursday letters has declined, precisely because of the unavoidable repetitions.

6. If however Paul had presided at the eucharist in the congregations he
founded, who had authorized him to do so? Certainly not "James and Cephas
and John, who were reputed to be pillars" (cf. Gal. 2:9). If the power to effec-
tuate the eucharist was bestowed as it were automatically by the appearance of
the risen Christ (1 Cor. 9:1, 15:8)—and how otherwise would James, the brother
of the Lord, who was not one of the "twelve." have been able to attain his position of all-embracing leadership of the Jerusalem community (Acts 12:17,
15:13, Gal. 1:19, 2:12)?—then would this not have to apply to all to whom the
risen Christ had shown himself and thus also to Mary Magdalen (John 20:11-
18) and the "more than five hundred brethren" (1 Cor. 15:6) who undoubtedly
included a number of "sisters"? This enables us to recognize the claim that
"only the ministerial priest" can "effectively speak that word through which
the eucharistic sacrifice, Christ's body and blood, becomes present" as a dogmatic construct that is both unpractical and remote from real life (Michael
Schmaus, *Der Glaube der Kirche*, vol. V section 3, St Ottilien ²1982, pp. 232-
33).

and the apostles also has the consequence that sayings directed at the "disciples" are restricted to priests. Thus the saying addressed to the seventy disciples: "The harvest is plentiful, but the labourers are few; pray therefore the Lord of the harvest to send out labourers into his harvest" (Luke 10:2) is naturally applied to the priesthood.[7]

Equally naturally the saying directed to the disciples setting out on their mission: "He who hears you, hears me, and he who rejects you rejects me" (Luke 10:16) is applied to the priesthood.[8] And the saying Jesus addressed to the "disciples": "If you forgive the sins of any, they are forgiven; if you retain the sins of any, they are retained" leads to the conclusion: "Priests, then, by the will of Christ, are the only ministers of the Sacrament of Reconciliation."[9]

From this presupposition depends a further element of the traditional image of the priest: the selection and raising up of the priest from among ordinary people. He is hardly a disciple

---

7. Pius XII, *Menti Nostrae*, *AAS* 42 (1950) p. 682. J. Ernst writes as follows in *Das Evangelium nach Lukas* (Regensburg 1977, pp. 330-1): "The relationship between the sending out of the twelve (Luke 9:1-6) and of the seventy-two (Luke 10:1-20) needs thinking about with regard to the editorial history of these passages. Luke is thinking in the first instance of Israel, which is represented by the twelve tribes, and secondarily of the whole world, which according to Genesis 10 in the Septuagint found its abundance in the seventy-two nations. The thought of the mission to the gentiles is thus partly responsible for the double narration. The historical background is to be looked for in the sending out of a larger number of disciples, among whom Luke singles out the representative groups of the seventy-two and of the twelve."

8. *Directory* § 16.

9. *Directory* § 51.   Rudolf Bultmann writes (*The Gospel of John: A Commentary*, Oxford 1971, p. 693): "It is self-evident that it is not a special apostolic authority that is imparted here, but that the community as such is equipped with this authority."   Rudolf Schnackenburg writes (*The Gospel according to St John*, vol. 3, London and New York 1982, p. 327): "In the evangelist's sense, a limitation to the 'eleven apostles' is not tenable. . . . A limitation of the authority to the disciples present or to later office-holders is far from the evangelist's mind; as up till now the disciples represent the Church, and in 1 John office-holders are not mentioned in connection with ecclesiastical practice." The extent to which the evangelist's intentions are contradicted if the power "to forgive and retain sins" is restricted to certain ministers has been demonstrated urgently and convincingly by M. Hasitschka, *Befreiung von Sünde nach dem Johannesevangelium*, Innsbruck 1989, pp. 402-22.

any longer but becomes almost a "second Christ". *Sacerdos alter Christus* is a saying common in Catholic usage. "So a cleric should be considered as a man chosen and set apart from the midst of the people, and blessed in a very special way with heavenly gifts—a sharer in divine power, and, to put it briefly, another Christ."[10] There is a predilection for quoting Hebrews 5:1 in this context: "For every high priest chosen from among men is appointed to act on behalf of men in relation to God." Nobody is bothered by the fact that appealing to this text is inappropriate on two counts. First, what it is dealing with is the Jewish high priest. Second, no New Testament writing comes down so decidedly against the idea of a Christian priesthood as the letter to the Hebrews (see pp. 67-68 below).

But this is not the end of it. The priest, chosen from among men, appointed for men, has to stand as a mediator between God and his fellow-men. The priestly office "makes the priest a mediator between God and man.[11] The scriptural justification for this is found in 1 Timothy 2:5: "For there is one God, and there is one mediator between God and men, the man Christ Jesus." Instead of concluding from this that there can be no other human mediator apart from the man Jesus Christ, the very opposite conclusion is drawn: the role of mediator that Christ holds belongs to the priest as "second Christ." Hence the sacrament of order stamps an inextinguishable mark (*character indelebilis*) on the priest. "Even the most lamentable downfall which, through human frailty, is possible to a priest can never blot out from his soul the priestly character."[12] And once again a biblical passage is used as a proof-text when it is not appropriate. It is the promise David makes after the conquest of Jerusalem to the Jebusite priest whom he takes on for the service of Yahweh: "You

---

10. Quoted by John XXIII in his encyclical *Sacerdotii Nostri Primordia* (§ 6) from a speech which his predecessor Pius XII was prevented by death from delivering. Cf. also Pius XI, *Ad Catholici Sacerdotii* § 37: "He [the priest] must live as a second Christ."

11. Pius XI, *Ad Catholici Sacerdotii* § 33.

12. Pius XI, *enc. cit.* § 22; John Paul II's letter to all the priests of the Church for Maundy Thursday 1990, § 1. For the *character indelebilis* see pp. 107-108 below.

are a priest for ever after the order of Melchizedek" (Ps. 110:4). The image of the priest suffers an additional inflation through the extension whereby every offence by a priest against the grave obligation of chastity "involves the added guilt of sacrilege."[13]

The transference of biblical statements about the Israelite and Jewish priesthood to the priesthood of the Church is not only wrong in terms of the history of religion, illogical, and methodologically untenable. It is also the cause of the entire mistaken development that we have had to endure until the present. For example, it takes completely for granted the presupposition that Jesus wanted a priesthood of this kind and thereby completely disregards the attitude of rejection that Jesus evinced towards the Temple priesthood (see below). So even the idea that the Old Testament priesthood simply acted as a model for the Christian priesthood could arise. Pius XI was admittedly full of praise for the Temple and Israel's pattern of worship. "It would seem that God, in His great care for them, wished to impress upon the still primitive mind of the Jewish people one great central idea," he wrote. "This idea throughout the history of the chosen people was to shed its light over all events, laws, ranks and offices: the idea of sacrifice and priesthood." But he does not hesitate to go on to cut this down to size: "Yet this ancient priesthood derived its greatest majesty and glory from being a foretype of the Christian priesthood; the priesthood of the New and eternal Covenant."[14]

Even the honorific title of office "pastor," "shepherd," rests ultimately on a biblical model. God is the shepherd of Israel (Ps. 80:1, Isa. 40:11, and frequently), and in the New Testament Jesus' concern for his own is likewise also described using the image of the shepherd (John 10). So the idea of adopting this designation for priests too suggested itself. Nevertheless, the surprising thing is that very recently, in what is said to be the age of the laity, a Roman document should see fit to reserve the title "pastor" exclusively for priests. It is the "ministerial priesthood of the presbyter," we read, "to which on the basis of ordi-

---

13. Pius XI, *Ad Catholici Sacerdotii* § 40.
14. *Enc. cit.* § 11.

nation received from the bishop the term 'pastor' in the proper and unequivocal sense can alone be attributed."[15] What are the laity meant to think, especially in the mission countries where for the past hundred and fifty years they have performed practically all the work of pastors?

As is to be expected, this vision of the priesthood is mirrored in spiritual writing. What never ceases to amaze is the unquestioning acceptance of Jesus' establishment of the priesthood as well as the smooth transition from the person of Jesus to the person of the priest, from what Jesus does to what the priest does. During my student days a classic work was the collection of addresses given by Bishop W. Stockums, auxiliary of Cologne and for many years director of the Leonine College in Bonn, published in 1934 under the title *The Priesthood*, a book marked by a deep sense of responsibility and wide experience. In this we read that, just like the Church, the Catholic priesthood arose not from temporal and earthly necessities but is of immediate divine origin: "It was not fashioned by the hand of man, but by the hand of God. Christ Himself, the eternal Son of God, is the one who called the priesthood into existence. He planted it in the world. . . . He alone is the founder of the New Testament priesthood."[16] In this he admittedly worked on existing elements, particularly the Israelite priesthood. But "He abolished systematically, and for all time, the entire Old Testament order of sacrifice; in place of those typical offerings which had accomplished their purpose, He set up a new and eternal sacrifice, the offering up of which He committed to the hands of new priests, called by Him."[17]

Corresponding to the theology of those years the priest is here too a second Christ: "As in his higher state of being, so also in his activity the priest is nothing else and nothing less than another Christ."[18] There is no question but that sayings in the sermon on the mount such as "You are the salt of the earth . . . You

15. *Directory* § 19.

16. Wilhelm Stockums, *The Priesthood*, St Louis/London 1938, p. 2.

17. *Ibid.*, p. 6.

18. *Ibid.*, p. 42.

are the light of the world . . ." (Matt. 5:13, 14) are directed to the apostles and thus to priests.[19]

Even in those days, when it came to gushing sentimental kitsch glorifying the priesthood in a manner virtually devoid of any contact with reality, we were not quite as uncritical as we were of Stockums' book on the priesthood and similar well-meant treatises and exhortations of this kind. An alarming example of this kind of thing is provided by Georg Thurmair:

> I would like to be God's priest: wear vestments that make me holy, speak the language that fulfils his spirit, pray the words that change the bread, and make sacrifices that are endured.
>
> I would like to be God's priest: bestow the blessing on his creation, live love and exist for thousands, take care of things and pray for thousands, live the faith and glow for thousands.
>
> I would like to be God's priest: ring the bells to make the towers rock, light fire to make heaven burn, open doors to make journeys reach their end, and consume myself to make mankind believe.[20]

Admittedly, as the crisis of the priesthood in our present century develops, the more reticent do statements on the priest-

---

19. *Ibid.*, pp. 65-70.
20.   Ich möchte Gottes Priester sein:
        Gewänder tragen, die mich heilig machen,
        Die Sprache reden, die sein Geist erfüllt,
        Die Worte beten, die das Brot verwandeln,
        Und Opfer heben, die erduldet sind.

        Ich möchte Gottes Priester sein:
        Den Segen spenden über Seine Schöpfung,
        Die Liebe leben und für Tausend sein,
        Die Sorge tragen und für Tausend beten,
        Den Glauben leben und für Tausend glühn.

        Ich möchte Gottes Priester sein:
        Die Glocken läuten, daß die Türme schwanken,
        Und Feuer zünden, daß der Himmel brennt,
        Die Tore öffnen, daß die Wege enden,
        Und mich verbrennen, daß die Menschheit glaubt.

   From G. Thurmair, *Die ersten Gedichte—an die Freunde*, Düsseldorf 1938, p. 61. There are twenty-five pieces by Thurmair in the contemporary hymnal *Gotteslob*.

hood become. Discussion increasingly focuses on questions of how one can still be a priest today, how one can give the priesthood a meaning, how one can live it in different social circumstances. For Bernhard Häring the questions are: What priests do we need? Does the contemporary model of the priest have any future at all? In Häring's view the present crisis of the clergy demands "growth, deepening, and also change."[21] In the case of observations of this kind the present structure of the Church is hardly ever called into question. Nevertheless Häring admits: "The Church of the first three centuries did not know . . . either the concept or the reality of a 'clergy'."[22] He traces the formation of classes of priests "separated from the ordinary people of the Church" back to the "Fall of the Constantinian era," especially since "in the gospels and the genuine epistles Jesus is never addressed as priest or indeed as 'high priest'."

Häring then suggests the possibility that "older men" ["*Senioren*"] could take over "the office of president at the celebration of the eucharist." "One does not need to be a prophet or visionary to predict that the Church will seize this opportunity. But what cannot be predicted is the extent of the damage the Church will still inflict on itself and its mission before the Church's highest leadership takes note of this."[23]

We need to justify and deepen this perspective exegetically and historically. In this the first thing evident is that for the first two hundred years it was not a rite of ordination but a commission that was the decisive criterion for presiding at the eucharist, and that a sacrament of priestly ordination—which, if a sacrament, must have been instituted by Christ—cannot be detected before the fifth century.

---

21. B. Häring, *Heute Priester sein. Eine kritische Ermutigung*, Freiburg-im-Breisgau ²1996, p. 77.

22. *Ibid.*, pp. 47-9.

23. *Ibid.*, pp. 106-7.

2: The Jewish priesthood at the time of Jesus

The effects of the crisis of the priesthood and of the Church's office of leadership are felt today in the remotest congregation. Catholics are confronted with the picture of a Church in distress. The shortage of priests, parishes deprived of the eucharist, celibacy, the ordination of women: these are the problems which, if not on their own, still to a considerable extent determine this state of affairs and are the subject of unceasing discussion, even if with only very modest results. It looks as if what is really the fundamental question is not brought into focus at all. Increasingly today "laypeople" are appointed to a pastoral ministry frequently equivalent to heading a congregation, while they are still not able to fulfil the central task of the leader of a congregation—celebrating the eucharist with the congregation. "Why therefore do we not ordain as priests and thus as fully competent leaders of congregations those who *de facto* already fulfil as much of the task of leading a congregation as possible and have to a considerable extent proved their competence in this task?" is the question continually raised.[24] The answer: this would go against the teaching of the Council.[25] In practical terms this means that a congregation either obtains an ordained leader and thus has access to the eucharist, or has a non-ordained leader and therefore has to do without the regular celebration of the eucharist. The bishops do not seem to be interested in the fact that in its history the Church has known other models, ones better justified on the basis of the New Testament, which would, in the alarming conditions of today, seem to be virtually an urgent imperative. What they are concerned about above all is "a renewed form of the priestly ministry."[26] But there are grounds for confidence: "The next step needed we should confidently leave to the continuing guidance of God's Holy Spirit."[27]

---

24. Walter Kasper, "Der Leitungsdienst in der Gemeinde. Studientag der Deutschen Bischofskonferenz," in *Reute*, 23 February 1994, p. 21.

25. *Ibid.*, p. 22. Cf. the resolution of the autumn plenary assembly of the Austrian bishops' conference, 8-10 November 1994, that it is only to an ordained priest that the bishop may entrust the task of heading a congregation (Herder-Korrespondenz 48 [1994], p. 648).

26. Kasper, *op. cit.* p. 22.

27. *Ibid.*, p. 22.

The Christian Church's priesthood under discussion has its roots in the Israelite and Jewish priesthood. The most obvious difference is that it does not involve any bloody sacrifice. Admittedly for Judaism from the end of the Babylonian exile onward (around 500 BC) the synagogue became the locus of prayer, the reading of scripture, and instruction. From then on it maintained Judaism both in the Jewish homeland and in the worldwide diaspora through the centuries. Nevertheless the Jerusalem Temple remained the religious centre of the nation. It was the goal of pilgrimage, especially at the three great feasts of Passover, the feast of weeks, and the feast of tabernacles, and not only for local Jews, but for pious Jews from all over the world. It was at the Temple that theology was taught; it was at the Temple that the worship that sustained the life of the people was conducted.

This was organized on very hierarchical lines. At the top was the High Priest, who was responsible for the entire conduct of worship. He was the only mortal who on one day a year, Yom Kippur, the Day of Atonement, was allowed to enter the Holy of Holies, the innermost part of the Temple, and thus was deemed worthy of direct encounter with Yahweh. But he was only to pray briefly there so that the people were not worried lest something should have befallen him.[28] In addition the High Priest presided over the sanhedrin, the supreme council, and thus wielded considerable political influence. He belonged to the Sadducees.

Supporting him were the "ordinary" priests. They were able to enter the Temple forecourts, where twice a day they burned incense. In the priests' forecourt, where the altar for burnt offerings stood, they conducted the sacrifices of animals and food. The priests' ministry was not a full-time job. They followed a secular vocation, since their duties involved them serving the Temple for a week at a time only twice a year.[29]

A third group of Temple personnel was formed by the Levites.

---

28. Joachim Jeremias, *Jerusalem in the Time of Jesus*, London 1969, pp. 149-50; Bo Ivar Reicke, *The New Testament Era*, London 1969, pp. 163-8.

29. Jeremias, *op. cit.*, pp. 198-207.

Their duties comprised all the ancillary fields of worship: doorkeeping, maintaining order, chant and music. Like the priests they too had their weeks of service. It is commonly assumed that three hundred priests and four hundred Levites were needed every day, so that a grand total of 7,200 priests and 9,600 Levites is reckoned with.[30]

It goes without saying that the butchery undertaken in the Temple was extremely unpleasant and gave rise to a ghastly stench, which was neutralized with incense (as is still common in the East today). What must have been particularly horrible was the slaughter of the paschal lambs, when the priests were wading ankle-deep in blood.[31] Even if the quarter of a million animal victims mentioned by Josephus is a vast exaggeration the total could well have been several tens of thousands. The Temple thus resembled an abattoir rather than a house of prayer.

However, it was not these bloody sacrifices as such that aroused the prophets' criticism. Rather they condemned the lack of consistency between zealously organized worship intended to fulfil religious duties and the justice and love of neighbour that were demanded. When the prophet Amos, around the middle of the eighth century BC, has Yahweh declaring: "I hate, I despise your feasts, and I take no delight in your solemn assemblies. Even though you offer me your burnt offerings and cereal offerings, I will not accept them, and the peace offerings of your fatted beasts I will not look upon" (Amos 5:21-2), the emphasis is on "your": it is a question of attitude. Given the way of life of those offering sacrifice, their sacrifices could not please God. Instead of these, what was needed was this: "But let justice roll down like waters, and righteousness like an ever-flowing stream" (5:24). If a later hand then goes on to put the penetrating question: "Did you bring to me sacrifices and offerings the forty years in the wilderness, O house of Israel?" (5:25) this shows that already in the sixth century BC animal sacrifice was being called into question, a development that was decisively encouraged during the Temple-less period of the Babylonian exile.

---

30. *Ibid.*, pp. 207-13.

31. "It is a matter of pride for the sons of Aaron to wade in blood up to their ankles" (Pes. 65b).

It was a question of shifting away from animal sacrifice to an ethically responsible fundamental attitude. Thus Psalm 50:7-15 is, if possible, even fiercer than Amos in judging the sacrifice of animals ("Do I eat the flesh of bulls, or drink the blood of goats? Offer to God a sacrifice of thanksgiving" vv. 13-14), while awareness of a spiritualized service of God and a longing for the sacrifice of the heart and the lips are witnessed by passages such as Psalm 40:6-8: "Sacrifice and offering thou dost not desire, but thou hast given me an open ear. . . . I delight to do thy will, O my God; thy law is within my heart"; or Psalm 51:16-17: "For thou hast no delight in sacrifice; were I to give a burnt offering thou wouldst not be pleased. The sacrifice acceptable to God is a broken spirit; a broken and contrite heart, O God, thou wilt not despise"; and Psalm 69:30-31: "I will praise the name of God with a song; I will magnify him with thanksgiving. This will please the Lord more than an ox or a bull with horns and hoofs."

There was thus already an ancient tradition and a profound awareness in the Jewish people, which Jesus was able to latch on to in his condemnation of the Temple sacrifices. "I desire mercy and not sacrifice"—this quotation from Hosea (6:6) cited twice by Matthew, with his delight in the law and in sacrifice, characterizes Jesus' shift from the sphere of ritual worship to that of morality.

How strongly this awareness had taken root in the Jewish world of Jesus' time has been shown by the writings of the Essene community of Qumran. The founder of the community seems to have been a priest of the Jerusalem Temple. So the Qumran community was organized on strict hierarchical lines according to the Temple model. The priests occupied a privileged position supported by the Levites, followed by the other members of the community (the "many"). But the group had broken with the Temple because in its eyes the latter was run by unworthy priests. From this there arose for the community a revolutionary new understanding of the Temple: it (the community) is itself God's sanctuary, it is a "holy house for Israel and a circle of the all-holiest for Aaron" (1QS VIII:5-6, cf. IX:6).

This transfer of Temple concepts to the community prepared the ground for the idea attested in the Pauline epistles and writings influenced by Paul (1 Cor. 3:16-17; 2 Cor. 6:16; 1 Cor 6:19; Eph. 2:19-22; 1 Peter 2:4-10; 1 Tim. 3:15) whereby it is the Christian community that is God's Temple. "The Christian reinterpretation of the Temple . . . was taken over from the Qumran community as an already developed idea."[32] Correspondingly the sacrifice that was offered in this temple is of a completely different kind. The community atones for Israel not "through the flesh of burnt offerings and the fat of sacrifices." Rather "the offering up of the lips as prescribed is like a sacrificial fragrance of righteousness, and complete transformation like a well-pleasing voluntary sacrifice" (1QS IX:4-5). In this it is striking how consciously the community follows the prophets' criticism of ritual worship and thus takes its place in an ancient tradition.[33] A similar exhortation is to be found in the letter to the Hebrews: "Through him then let us continually offer up a sacrifice of praise to God, that is, the fruit of lips that acknowledge his name" (Heb. 13:15).

Even if it sprang from a situation of distress and emergency, the reinterpretation of worship by the Qumran community, the replacement of the sacrifices of the Temple by the sacrifice of praise and conversion of life to the right path, became a singular event in the history of religion. It was to take on undreamed-of dimensions through its reinforcement by Jesus for the infant Church and through the destruction of the Temple for Judaism.

3: Jesus and the Temple

According to John Jesus went to Jerusalem five times and did so on feasts that attracted pilgrims: three Passovers (John 2:13, 23; 6:4; 11:25; 12:1), once for the feast of Tabernacles (7:2), and once for an un-named feast (5:1).[34] This would seem to show great zeal for the Temple, but in reality it does not represent

---

32. Georg Klinzing, *Die Umdeutung des Kultus in der Qumrangemeinde und im Neuen Testament*, Göttingen 1971, pp. 167-213, here 167-8.

33. Bertil Gärnter, *The Temple and the Community of Qumran and the New Testament*, Cambridge 1965, pp. 16-46, esp. 44-6.

34. Meinrad Limbeck, "Die Religionen im Neuen Testament," in *Theologische Quartalschrift* 169 (1989), pp. 44-56, here 48-51.

even a minimum. Every man—and to this day that means every male Jew from the completion of his thirteenth year—was bound to undertake the pilgrimage to Jerusalem three times a year: at Passover, at the feast of Weeks, and at the feast of Tabernacles (Ex. 23:17; 34:23; Deut. 16:16: "Three times a year all your males shall appear before the Lord your God. . . . They shall not appear before the Lord empty-handed"). Jesus does not seem to have kept to this commandment: at all events his doing so is not mentioned in the Gospels.

However, the point is not only how often Jesus visited the Temple. Still more important is what he did there. The commandment "They shall not appear before the Lord empty-handed" (Deut. 16:16, cf. Ex. 23:15, 34:20) was interpreted in Jesus' time to mean that every pilgrim had to bring two offerings: a burnt offering (*'olah, holocaustum*) for God (cattle, goat, sheep . . .) and a cereal offering (*shelamim*), which provided a celebratory meal for him and his family. The animals for sacrifice had to be handed over to the priest in the men's court with the man placing his hands on the animal he was offering.[35] It is nowhere said that Jesus took part in these rites, and never that he took part in a Temple service of worship. It is presumably making things too simple to say that this would have been something taken for granted for a "pious" Jew.[36] Nor do we know what his attitude to the Passover was. Biblical experts argue over whether his last supper was a Passover meal or a simple farewell meal. The latter would seem to be probable.[37]

Jesus' attitude and relationship to the priesthood seem to have been marked by considerable distance. Clear criticism of the priests and Levites can be discerned in the parable of the good Samaritan (Luke 10:30-7). Nor can any recognition of the Tem-

---

35. *Ibid.*, p. 48. For what follows see Ferdinand Hahn, *The Worship of the Early Church*, Philadelphia 1973, esp. pp. 23-5.

36. Limbeck, *art. cit.*, p. 48.

37. Cf. Thomas Söding, "Das Mahl des Herrn," in B. J. Hilberath and D. Sattler (ed.), *Vorgeschmack.. Festschrift für Th. Schneider*, Mainz 1995, p. 146: "It cannot be recognized that the most ancient tradition described a Passover meal of Jesus." For an account of the latest research see Paul F. Bradshaw, *The Search for the Origins of Christian Worship*, London 1992, pp. 30-55.

ple and its priesthood be read out of Jesus' instruction to healed
lepers to show themselves to the priests (Mark 1:40-4 and parallels; Luke 17:12-19), since with regard to lepers the priests had
legal functions, and it was only through their verdict that the
imposed separation from the community could be lifted.[38]

Finally, Jesus' threats of the imminent destruction of the Temple should not be overlooked. They are transmitted in six separate passages in the New Testament. That betokens their historicity and at the same time makes it impossible to derive them
all from a single original (Mark 13:2, 14:58, 15:29; Matt. 21:61;
Acts 6:14; John 2:19).[39]

When Jesus announces that he will rebuild the destroyed Temple in three days,[40] this can only mean the absolute end of the
Jerusalem Temple and of any earthly temple at all, and indeed
not just of the Temple as a building but of it as it functioned in
the way Jesus had experienced it. This kind of temple people no
longer needed. The temple Jesus proposed in its place was "not
made with hands" (Mark 14:58): it was of another order of being. In the Gospels this aspect is most strongly emphasized by
John, not without reference to Christian worship and the
eucharist: "But he spoke of the temple of his body" (John 2:21).
Although the idea of the community as the temple of God (see
above) was certainly known to John's Gospel, here therefore Jesus' body is understood as the true temple. "In place of the Jewish Temple worship comes that worship in which the crucified
and risen One assumes the central place which the Temple holds
in Jewish worship."[41]

Jesus underlined what he meant with the symbolic action of
driving the traders out of the Temple. One thing is common to
all four gospel versions (Mark 11:15-17; Matt. 21:12-17; Luke
19:45-48; John 2:12-17): the expulsion of those selling animals
and the action against the money-changers.[42] That can only have

---

38. Hahn, *op. cit.*, p. 23-4.

39. *Ibid.*, p. 26-7.

40. It is irrelevant here whether the "three days" go back to Jesus himself.

41. Oscar Cullmann, *Early Christian Worship*, London 1953, p. 73. For the
liturgical keynote of the whole of John's Gospel see below (pp. 00-00).

42. Bruce Chilton, *The Temple of Jesus*, University Park 1992, p. 100.

been directed against the Temple practice of sacrifice.[43] What is involved is more than the elimination of abuse, as a widespread misconception would have it. If Jesus drives out those buying and selling animals and overturns the tables of the money-changers—all of which was necessary for the conduct of sacrifices—then he makes the whole traditional ritual of sacrifice impossible, he proclaims it to be over and done with.[44]

This interpretation has been followed by more than one commentator. So Eduard Schweizer remarks of Luke's version: "The cleansing of the temple is reduced to the barest minimum; it leaves room for Jesus' daily teaching." In place of ritual worship we have Jesus' teaching, "which gives the temple its meaning, a meaning that it will also annul."[45] And on Jesus' forbidding the Temple's sacred vessels to be put on display Meinrad Limbeck asks us to bear this consideration in mind: "Jesus stood in the way of those who wanted to influence and inspire the people with the splendour of ritual. 'And he taught, and said to them' (v. 17). . . . In the place of ritual, in which the priests turned the faithful into spectators, Jesus places teaching—his teaching." But in doing so, according to Jewish thought of that time, Jesus removed the foundation not just from ritual worship but from the very existence of the people. One should indeed bear in mind "that the Temple ritual was genuinely for Israel a heavenly gift through which God wished to save his people from the consequences of their sins and trespasses. . . . When Jesus started driving the traders and buyers out of the Temple and when he overturned the tables of the money-changers and of the pigeon-sellers, then he was offending against the only thing that could secure the continued existence of the people of God."[46]

It is obvious that by doing this Jesus was bound to turn the Temple priesthood into his arch-enemies. Hence in the gospel

43. The fact that people could bring their animals for sacrifice with them or buy them elsewhere is irrelevant.

44. Limbeck, *art. cit.* p. 48; Thomas Söding, "Die Tempelaktion Jesu," in *Trierer Theologische Zeitschrift* 101 (1992) pp. 36-64, here 46.

45. Eduard Schweizer, *The Good News According to Luke*, London/Atlanta 1984, pp. 301-2.

46. Limbeck, *Markus-Evangelium*, Stuttgart ²1985, pp. 164-8.

accounts of the Passion the High Priests are unanimously named in the first place among Jesus' opponents who are seeking to have him arrested, handed over to the Romans, and executed. It is the chief priests and the scribes who are seeking to arrest him and kill him (Mark 14:1 and parallels). Judas Iscariot goes to the chief priests in order to betray Jesus to them (Mark 14:10 and parallels). It is with a crowd "from the chief priests and the scribes and the elders" that Judas arrives to have Jesus arrested (Mark 14:43 and parallels). One of Jesus' disciples strikes "the slave of the high priest" (Mark 14:47 and parallels). Jesus is taken first of all before the high priest (Mark 14:53 and parallels). The high priest leads the sanhedrin to condemn Jesus as deserving death (Mark 14:63-4 and parallels). It is to one of the high priest's maid-servants that Peter denies Jesus (Mark 14:66-72 and parallels). The chief priests and with them the entire sanhedrin hand Jesus over to Pilate (Mark 15:1 and parallels). The chief priests accuse Jesus before Pilate (Mark 15:3 and parallels) and stir the crowd up to demand his crucifixion (Mark 15:11 and parallels). The chief priests mock him when he is crucified (Mark 15:31 and parallels). And according to Matthew it is the chief priests once again who go to Pilate to ask for a guard to be put on the grave (Matt. 27:62-5) and who gave the soldiers money to say that Jesus' disciples had stolen his corpse (Matt. 28:11-15).

Hence today it is the generally held view that the Temple priesthood was responsible for Jesus' death. And since these were recruited from among the Sadducees, it was the Sadducees and not the Pharisees who handed Jesus over to die on the cross.[47]

The evangelists do not say anything about Jesus taking part in the worship of the Temple. But on the other hand it is important for them that he attended worship in the synagogue, worship that was simply what today we would call a service of the Word, and that he took an active part in it (Luke 4:16 ff.). It was a revolutionary event when, in the Temple-less period of the Babylonian exile, this new form of worship emerged spontane-

---

47. "Les prêtres en chef et le grand prêtre, qui étaient Sadducéens, sont les responsables de la mort de Jésus" (J. Le Moyne, *Les Sadducéens*, Paris 1972, p. 404).

ously, consisting of prayer and teaching without any sacrifice. This prepared Judaism for a later age when it would have to shape its worship from praise and thanksgiving, teaching and chant, without any Temple and without any sacrifice. Even when after the exile the Temple was rebuilt on the ruins of the old and the ritual worship of sacrifice was reinstated it did not have the field to itself any more. The worship of the synagogue was incomparably better suited to the needs of native Jewry and even more to those of the diaspora. In Jesus' time every major Jewish community not just in Palestine but throughout the Mediterranean basin had its own synagogue.

Synagogue worship "was the first that, with the ties with sacrifice completely broken, could be described as worship with the heart (*'abodah shel balleb*). But it had also liberated itself from all other formalities, from special consecrated places of worship and priests and indeed from all accessories: it was a purely spiritual form of worship and could easily spread throughout the entire world, since all that was needed to establish it was the will of a relatively small community. It was moreover the first form of worship that took place with great regularity: it was held not only on Sabbaths and feast-days but on all the days of the year, and so it bestowed on the whole of life a profound consecration, which became all the more permanent considering that daily prayer at morning and evening had already through the custom of the community become the usual practice of the individual, even if he did not find himself among the community."[48]

If this survey by the expert on the subject is correct, then synagogue worship must have corresponded wholly and entirely to Jesus' intentions. No wonder, therefore, that he made the synagogue his favourite place for teaching. He taught in the synagogue in his hometown of Nazareth (Luke 4:15) but also in that at Capernaum (Mark 1:21) and in synagogues generally (Matt. 4:23, 9:35, and parallels). Because it was exclusively teaching that he was concerned with he even turned the Temple, that house

---

48. I. Elbogen, *Der jüdische Gottesdienst in seiner geschichtlichen Entwicklung*, Frankfurt am Main ³1931, reprinted Hildesheim 1962, pp. 1-2.

of slaughter, into his house of teaching. Again and again the gospel tradition bears witness to him teaching in the Temple. "And he was teaching daily in the Temple" (Luke 19:47), "Jesus went up into the Temple and taught" (John 7:14, cf. 7:28, 8:20). To those who arrested him he responded: "Day after day I was with you in the Temple teaching" (Mark 14:49). Asked about his teaching by the chief priest, he answered, "I have always taught in synagogues and in the Temple" (John 18:20). Jesus could not have expressed his lack of interest in ritual sacrifice more clearly. In its place came the proclamation of the Word.

Jesus' conversation with the Samaritan woman (John 4) is particularly informative for his new understanding of worship. Talking to her he defined it as worship "in spirit and truth" linked neither to Zion, the holy mountain of the Jews, nor to Gerizim, the holy mountain of the Samaritans (John 4:21-24). Its core is the Word alone, and for John this is synonymous with the person of Jesus (John 1:14). Indeed, one of the chief concerns of the entire gospel according to John is to establish the relationship between primitive Christian worship and the historical life of Jesus.[49] The worship of the Christian community at the time of the evangelist is what Jesus wanted. In no case can this worship be a continuation of the priestly worship in the Temple.[50]

Particularly enlightening in this context is Jesus' saying about new wine and old wineskins: "And no one puts new wine into old wineskins; if he does, the wine will burst the skins, and the wine is lost, and so are the skins; but new wine is for fresh skins" (Mark 2:22 and parallels). Jesus warns against understanding what he is doing as merely a correction of Jewish religion to date. What is new cannot simply be integrated into what is old.[51]

Consequently Jesus also declared null and void the dogmatic distinction between clean and unclean that determines and disturbs Jewish thinking up to the present day. Nothing that goes into a man is unclean, only what comes out of his heart (cf. Mark

49. Cullmann, *Early Christian Worship*, pp. 57-59.

50. Cf. *ibid.*, pp. 73-4.

51. Ferdinand Hahn, *The Worship of the Early Church*, Philadelphia 1973, pp. 13-14.

7:15).[52] Jesus abolishes the boundary between the sacred and the profane. For him all that matters is the heart, is people's attitude and disposition. In this his teaching is similar to other great religions, such as Buddhism, which see the core of every religious attitude in the heart of man.

There is still another aspect that should not be overlooked in this context: the imminent expectation of the end of the world. Jesus' attitude to the Temple and its pattern of worship cannot be separated from this. He was expecting God's kingdom to break in with power in the immediate future. "Truly, I say to you, there are some standing here who will not taste death before they see the kingdom of God come with power" (Mark 9:1). This saying must go back to Jesus himself, since forty years after his death it could no longer come from the community as it had been overtaken by events. But if Jesus was convinced that the end of the world was nigh he could not have thought of building up or even planning an ecclesiastical system, an order of worship and a hierarchy.

Since, thanks to Jewish influence, thinking in terms of classes very soon found its way even into the community of Jesus' disciples, Matthew warns his community: "But you are not to be called rabbi, for you have one teacher, and you are all brethren" (Matt. 23:8). The community of Jesus' disciples could continue to exist only "if they were extremely consistent in resisting in their life all patterns that could encourage them to forget that their only teacher is Christ and their only father God."[53]

For Paul too Jesus' sacrifices in the Temple have lost their function. In the cross of Christ he sees the atonement and expiatory sacrifice set up between heaven and earth (Rom. 3:25).[54] If in addition one takes into consideration that it is generally accepted

---

52. "The man who denies that impurity from external sources can penetrate into man's essential being is striking at the presuppositions and the plain verbal sense of the Torah and at the authority of Moses himself. Over and above that he is striking at the presuppositions of the whole classical concept of cultus with its sacrificial and expiatory system" (E. Käsemann, quoted by Hahn, *op. cit.*, p. 17).

53. Limbeck, *Matthäus-Evangelium*, p. 267.

54. K. H. Schelkle, *Meditationen über den Römerbrief*, Einsiedeln 1962, p. 61.

that here Paul is working on the basis of an older Palestinian tradition concerned not just with Jesus' death but also with the last supper,[55] what is completely new about Christian worship as opposed to that of the Temple appears in all the clearer a light.

In the event the sacrifice that is expected of Christians is for Paul of a quite different kind: "I appeal to you . . . to present your bodies as a living sacrifice, holy and acceptable to God, which is your spiritual worship (*logike latreia*)" (Rom. 12:1). Perhaps we could be so bold as to translate *logike latreia* by "service of the Word." In any case Paul places Christian worship in emphatic contrast to Jewish. Christians are to bring their bodies (not the bodies of animals) as a living sacrifice (instead of dead animals). True worship is the offering of one's body and of one's life.

What is meant by *logike latreia* is made clear by the parallel passage in 1 Peter 2:5, which speaks of *pneumatikai thusiai*, of "spiritual sacrifices" and "living stones" to be built into a spiritual house. The Christian offers his or her body, not his or her soul.

Paul nevertheless goes further. Worship for him is not just offering the body but above all the proclamation of the gospel. With great emphasis the apostle speaks of the liturgical worship of the gospel which he fulfils. In Romans 1:9 he declares that "with my spirit" he serves in the gospel of Christ. What is meant by this is not that Paul understands himself as a priest in the proclamation of the gospel. Rather this proclamation takes the place of the ritual worship of the Temple. Paul uses here the word *latreuo*, which in the Septuagint and in the New Testament is used of the Jewish worship of the Temple, and relates it to the gospel.

Even more significant is Romans 15:16 where Paul describes himself as *leitourgos Christou Iesou*, "a minister of Christ Jesus to the Gentiles in the priestly service of the gospel of God, so that the offering of the Gentiles may be acceptable." With this he turns the entire terminology of Jewish worship upside down:

---

55. O. Michel, *Der Brief an die Römer*, Göttingen ⁴1966; J. Blank. in P. Eicher, *Neues Handbuch Theologischer Grundbegriffe* IV, Munich 1991, p. 373.

priestly ministry consists of the proclamation of the gospel. The sacrificial offerings are the Gentiles who have been won for the gospel.[56]

4: The earliest Christian form of worship

(1) Eating with the Risen Lord

So from the very beginning Christian worship was radically different from Jewish. Admittedly Acts bears witness to the fact that the Aramaic-speaking core community in Jerusalem continued to hold on to the traditional forms of Jewish devotion, especially after James, the brother of the Lord, had take over sole responsibility for running the Jerusalem community. They attended the Temple (whether they took part in its worship is, as in the case of Jesus, not said), observed the dietary laws, practised circumcision.[57] To this was already added the "breaking of bread" in their own houses. Opposition to them grew from the Greek-speaking Jewish Christians, the "Hellenists." Their powerful spokesman Stephen was accused by the Jews of never ceasing to speak against the Temple and the law (Acts 6:13-14). But it was quite certainly these Hellenists who disrupted the confined narrowness of the Aramaic Jewish Christian community. It is them we have to thank for the fact that Jesus' religion was able to become a universal religion in which there was neither sacrifice nor circumcision nor dietary laws.

In this way Christian worship was distinguished from Jewish as day is from night. It took place not in sacred but in profane surroundings. There is no talk of priests and sacrifices. Even when Temple priests joined the band of Jesus' disciples they did not appear as such. The objection can of course be raised that a new form of Jewish worship, without the Temple and sacrifices, had already been prepared by the worship of the synagogues,

---

56. Hahn, *op. cit.*, p. 35. It is no obstacle to this that Judaism already knew a spiritualization of the terminology of sacrifice (see pp. 48-50 above) and that the same expression *'abodah* was used for prayer and preaching as for the service of the altar (Michel, *Der Brief an die Römer*, on 15:16).

57. Limbeck, "Die Religionen im Neuen Testament," (note 34 above), pp. 51-2.

which consisted simply of a service of the Word. However, the original Christian form of worship is once again not simply a service of the Word. Rather a decisive role is played by the meal, an aspect alien to the worship of the synagogue. For these meals the distinctive term "the breaking of bread" was used, a term that hardly occurs in ordinary secular Greek but which rather finds its context in Jewish custom. In the Gospels it describes a typical gesture of Jesus, both in the accounts of the feeding of the five thousand (Mark 6:41) and of the four thousand (Mark 8:6), where the story is already taking on a liturgical tinge, and in the account of the last supper (Mark 14:22: "He took bread, and blessed, and broke it, and gave it to them," and similarly in all four accounts of the institution of the eucharist). This same turn of phrase is to be found in the story of Jesus' meal with his disciples at Emmaus (Luke 24:30).

In these celebratory meals the primitive community was clearly making the connection with the meals which Jesus held with his disciples, especially after his resurrection.[58] In place of the presence of Yahweh in the Temple we now have the presence of the risen Lord. He is and remains the now invisible host. He presides over the meal. In this we should remember that especially in the understanding of Eastern peoples the host does not merely supply his guests with food and drink: he gives them above all his presence and thus himself.[59]

This connection between the resurrection and the Lord's Supper is emphasized particularly in Peter's speech at Caesarea: "But God raised him [Jesus] on the third day and made him manifest; not to all the people but to us who were chosen by God as witnesses, who ate and drank with him after he rose from the dead" (Acts 10:40-1). While the new-born community still went to pray in the Temple, it was "alternately in their homes" (*kat'*

---

58. Cullmann, *Early Christian Worship*, pp. 14-16.

59. Cf. for a detailed discussion Thomas Söding, "Das Mahl des Herrn," (note 37 above). The Christian Churches would have saved themselves a great deal of bickering up till the present if they had refrained from discussing the manner in which Jesus is present in the eucharist. If we could merely agree that we are simply having a meal with him as his disciples did and that he is present at this then all dispute would be at an end.

oikon) that they held their celebratory meal, and did so with "exultation" (*agalliasis*), a word that could almost be translated as "exuberant joy" (Acts 2:46).[60]

The extent to which these eucharistic celebratory meals took place against the background of the resurrection is also shown by the day on which they took place. We do admittedly learn from Acts of people meeting daily in their houses (Acts 2:46). But this happened chiefly on the first day of the week (Acts 20:7, 1 Cor. 16:2), which was also called "the Lord's day" (Rev. 1:10, and cf. the Apostolic Fathers, e.g. *Didache* 14:1). In deliberate distinction to Judaism "the first Christians selected the first day of the week, since on this day Christ had risen from the dead, and on this day he had appeared to the disciples gathered together for a meal."[61] So for them every Lord's day is a celebration of Easter.

(2) The eucharist in the Didache

Outside the New Testament this Christian celebratory meal is first attested by the *Teaching of the Twelve Apostles* or *Didache* and by Justin Martyr. The *Didache* is a manual of Christian instruction written in Greek around the beginning of the second century, intended for practical use and reflecting the practice of the Christian community; in it very archaic Jewish Christian traditions can be traced. It is thought to originate from the region of Syria and Palestine.

Of the two parts into which this tract falls it is the second that is relevant here, and particularly the instructions about the community's celebratory meal (9:1-10:7). These provide the oldest order of service known to us for the Christian eucharist and are therefore of fundamental importance for its history.[62] Their one limitation is that presumably they applied only to a particular local Church.

---

60. Cullmann, *op. cit.*, pp. 9-10, 15.

61. Cullmann, *op. cit.*, pp. 10-11; Willy Rordorf, *Sunday: the history of the day or rest and worship in the earliest centuries of the Christian Church*, London 1968, and his chapter "La célébration de la Sainte Cène dans l'Église ancienne," in *Liturgie, foi et vie des premiers chrétiens*, Paris 1986, pp. 59-71.

62. For what follows see above all Kurt Niederwimmer, *Die Didache*, Göttingen ²1993, pp. 173-209.

Understanding of these instructions is made more difficult by the fact that they do not contain a complete form of service but merely certain definite prayers, which do not form part of the celebratory meal itself. They consist of prayers before and after the meal, of a clearly Jewish stamp. They also use the term "eucharist" for this Christian service of worship, for the first time in an early Christian document.

The prayer before the meal is as follows:[63]

> And concerning the eucharist, hold eucharist (or give thanks) thus:
> First concerning the cup:[64]
> "We give thanks to thee, our Father,
> for the holy vine of David thy child,
> which thou didst make known to us through Jesus thy child;
> to thee be glory for ever."
> And concerning the broken bread:
> "We give thee thanks, our Father,
> for the life and knowledge which thou didst make known to us
> through Jesus thy child.
> To thee be glory for ever.
> As this broken bread was scattered upon the mountains,
> but was brought together and became one,
> so let thy Church be gathered together
> from the ends of the earth into thy kingdom,
> for thine is the glory and the power
> through Jesus Christ for ever."
> But let none eat or drink of your eucharist
> except those who have been baptized in the Lord's name.
> For concerning this also did the Lord say,
> "Give not that which is holy to the dogs."

---

63. The translation is that by Kirsopp Lake, *The Apostolic Fathers*, Loeb Classical Library, London/Cambridge, Mass., 1912, vol. I pp. 323 ff.

64. The blessing of the cup before the bread does not correspond to the custom "at a Jewish meal when guests were entertained" (Niederwimmer, *op. cit.*, p. 181) at which the cup was only blessed after the meal whereas before the meal it was only the bread, as in Luke's and Paul's accounts of the Last Supper. The sequence wine/bread is found only on the sabbath eve and on feast days (at kiddush), which would once again confirm that for the Jewish Christian community the Lord's day took the place of the earlier sabbath.

The instructions for giving thanks after the meal are as follows:

> But after you are satisfied with food, thus give thanks:
> "We give thanks to thee, O Holy Father,
> for thy holy name which thou didst make
> to tabernacle in our hearts,
> and for the knowledge and faith and immortality
> which thou didst make known to us through Jesus thy child.
> To thee be glory for ever.
> Thou, Lord Almighty,
> didst create all things for thy name's sake,
> and didst give food and drink to men for their enjoyment,
> that they might give thanks to thee,
> but us thou has blessed with spiritual food and drink
> and eternal light through thy child.
> Above all we give thanks to thee
> for that thou art mighty.
> To thee be glory for ever.
> Remember, Lord, thy Church, to deliver it from all evil
> and to make it perfect in thy love,
> and gather it together in its holiness from the four winds
> to thy kingdom which thou hast prepared for it.
> For thine is the power and the glory for ever.
> Let grace come and let this world pass away.
> Hosannah to the God of David.
> If any man be holy, let him come.
> If any man be not, let him repent.
> Maranatha.   Amen.

But what kind of a meal was it that was preceded and followed by these two prayers? Certainly it was a meal in the full sense of satisfying one's hunger. Nonetheless, it is difficult to see it as a eucharistic meal. There is no reference to institution by Jesus, to his body and blood, to his death.[65] On the other hand the exhortation at the end of the thanksgiving: "If any man be holy,

---

65. Admittedly H. J. Vogt writes (*Theologische Quartalschrift* 175 [1995], p. 194: "an account of the Last Supper was not compulsory."

let him come" (10:6) is difficult to understand other than as an invitation to the eucharistic meal.[66]

However, the possibility that the actual meal to which these prayers before and after belong was itself the eucharistic meal cannot be excluded.[67] The word *eucharistia* used in the introduction to the prayers before the meal and in the note after it is not decisive for this understanding, since it can be understood in a more comprehensive sense than contemporary ecclesiastical usage as a heading or description for the entire celebration. Nevertheless in either case there remains the riddle of the complete silence about the eucharistic meal itself. What was said, how did it proceed, who presided at it? "Here therefore there is still an open problem."[68] What in any case is unambiguous is that the service of worship found in the *Didache* consists essentially of a meal, the conduct of which was a matter for the community. There is no talk of any president.

Finally, there is the instruction in 14:1: "On the Lord's day come together, break bread and hold eucharist (give thanks), after confessing your transgressions that your offering may be pure." From this is deduced that the eucharist is understood as a sacrifice in the *Didache*. However, the context of this instruction is not the eucharist: rather the subject is confession and reconciliation. The phrase "that your offering (*thusia*, sacrifice) may be pure" presupposes that one has already acknowledged one's transgressions. It refers to the prayers said at the time:

---

66. Willy Rordorf, in Rordorf and André Tuilier, *La Doctrine des Douze Apôtres*, Paris 1978 (*Sources chrétiennes* 248), pp. 38-48; "L'eucharistie des premiers chrétiens," in his *Liturgie* (note 61 above), pp. 187-208; *Die Mahlgebete in Didache Kap. 9-10* (at press); Niederwimmer, *op. cit.*, pp. 173-80.

67. Thus Klaus Wengst: "The eucharist is a meal that satisfies hunger, and the meal that satisfies hunger at which these prayers were spoken is a eucharist" (*Didache [Apostellehre], Barnabasbrief, Zweiter Klemensbrief, Schrift an Diognet*, Darmstadt 1984, p. 45). John W. Riggs ("The Sacred Food in *Didache* 9-10 and Second-Century Ecclesiologies," in Clayton N. Jefford [ed.], *The Didache in Context*, supplement to *Novum Testamentum* 77, Leiden 1995, pp. 256-83) also refuses to make a sharp distinction between the two. Ludwig A. Winterswyl (*Die Zwölfapostellehre. Eine urchristliche Gemeindeordnung*, Freiburg-im-Breisgau ²1954) places the eucharistic communion before the actual meal (p. 63). For the latest state of the discussion see Rordorf, *Mahlgebete*.

68. Niederwimmer, *op. cit.*, p. 182.

these are to be a pure offering,[69] with offering of course being understood in a spiritual sense.

It is worth noting once more that no minister makes his appearance in this entire celebration. One might look for these among the (itinerant or settled) "prophets" and "teachers." But in addition the community is urged to augment their (obviously declining) numbers by established ministers, bishops and deacons, and to pay them the same respect as prophets and teachers. "Appoint (elect) therefore for yourselves bishops and deacons worthy of the Lord, meek men, and not lovers of money, and truthful and approved, for they also minister to you the ministry of the prophets and teachers" (15:1).

This allows the suspicion that the bishops and deacons initially had difficulty in gaining recognition in comparison with the prophets and teachers. They were settled in one place and, in contrast to the prophets and teachers, they were responsible for their own keep and thus clearly exercised a secular profession. From their functions in worship "a contrast between 'ministers' and 'laity' should not be deduced."[70] Responsibility and decision remained above all with the community. The bishops and deacons were elected by the community. "The *Didache* is not aware of any developed hierarchy: leadership functions have not yet been institutionalized, and the highest court of appeal in the community is the community itself."[71]

(3) Worship in Justin

A different situation emerges in the middle of the second century with the apologist and martyr Justin. He came from the Roman-Palestinian city of Flavia Neapolis.[72] He became a philosopher, but came to realize that Christianity was the only genuinely reliable and useful philosophy. So, availing himself of the technique of a pagan philosopher, he can venture to defend the

---

69. Wengst, *op. cit.*, pp. 53-7.

70. *Ibid.*, p. 42.

71. *Ibid.*, p. 36; cf. also Hans von Campenhausen, *Ecclesiastical Authority and Spiritual Power in the Church of the First Three Centuries*, London 1969, pp. 71-3.

72. Today Nablus, the largest Arab city in Israel.

Christian faith against the accusations of the pagans in an *apologia*[73] addressed to the Roman emperor and to debate with Judaism in the *Dialogue with Trypho*. In his *apologia* Justin offers a twofold description of the eucharist: first that which follows the rite of baptism (cf. 65), and then the Sunday eucharist (ch. 67). He describes the Sunday eucharist as follows:

> And on the day that is called the day of the sun a gathering takes place of all living in the towns or in the fields, and the memoirs of the apostles or the writings of the prophets are read as long as necessary. Then when the reader has finished the president gives an address exhorting and inviting those present to imitate this good example. Then we all stand up together and pray; and as I said earlier when we have stopped praying bread and wine and water are brought forth; and the president utters prayers and thanksgivings to the best of his ability, and the people gives its assent by saying "Amen"; and the distribution to each and the sharing of the eucharistic gifts [*ton eucharistethenton*] takes place, and is sent to those who are absent by the deacons. Those who are well off and so wish give what they will, each according to his discretion; and the collection is put down by the president, who uses it to help orphans and widows, those absent because of illness or for some other reason, those in prison, and to foreign visitors; quite simply, he becomes the guardian of those in need.

The entire celebration is conducted by a president (*proestos*) who also gives the address during the service of the Word that precedes the eucharist. There is no mention here either of an account of the institution of the eucharist.[74] Immediately after the prayers and thanksgivings, distribution is made from the "eucharistic gifts" (*ton eucharistethenton*) and brought to those absent by the deacons.

---

73. It is usual to talk of two *apologias*, but these originally formed a single text.

74. Admittedly in the transitional chapter 66 Justin does give a free account of the institution of the eucharist, possibly from memory, as scriptural proof that the eucharist is truly Christ's body and blood. "In fact . . . with these words we seem to have the unintentional transmission of a liturgical formula, probably from the Roman Church" (O. Perler, "Logos und Eucharistie nach Justinus I. Apol. c. 66," in *Sapientia et Caritas. Gesammelte Aufsätze*, Fribourg 1990, pp. 471-91: this quotation is from p. 477).

Justin nevertheless leaves no doubt that the "eucharistic gifts" are the body and blood of the Lord (*sarx* and *haima*). However, he regards the eucharist as a commemoration, a memorial of the death of Jesus. But since at the same time he sees in it the fulfilment of the pure sacrifice universally offered that was promised by the prophet Malachi (1:10-12),[75] the eucharist itself inevitably becomes a sacrifice. This is a subject for further reflection. It is of fundamental importance for the development of the ideology of the priesthood.

(4) The unpriestly letter to the Hebrews

What characterized Christian worship of the first century was proclamation of the Word and offering of one's life in place of ritual sacrifice and priesthood, but also essentially a community meal with the risen Lord. What is surprising is that a New Testament document from toward the end of this century, the letter to the Hebrews, seems to be aware of only the one, not the other. Of all the writings of the New Testament, no other offers so decided a rejection of all priesthood after Christ.

The document is addressed to a Jewish Christian community having difficulties with its faith, a community in which possibly a certain nostalgia for Judaism and its Temple and ritual was spreading. So the author contrasts the old order with the new order that has dawned with Jesus. The old covenant has been superseded by the new. This replacement applies above all to the priesthood. The variable priesthood of the old covenant is contrasted with the once-and-for-all nature of Jesus' priesthood. As high priest Christ entered "the greater and more perfect tent, not made with hands" (9:11), leading those who believe in him like a liturgical procession "to Mount Zion and to the city of the living God, the heavenly Jerusalem, . . . and to the assembly of the first-born who are enrolled in heaven" (12:22-3), of which the old form of worship was merely a foreshadowing (9:9, 10:1-2). By offering himself Jesus has completed his work. This means that from now on there can no longer be any other sacri-

---

75. Charles Munier, *L'Apologie de Saint Justin, Philosophe et Martyr*, Fribourg 1994, pp. 135-41.

fice and at the same time any priesthood (7:27, 9:12, 10:11-18).[76]

Faced with so "unpriestly" an understanding of worship, it is hardly surprising that the letter to the Hebrews also presents a thoroughly "unpriestly" way of running the Christian community. As a little later with Justin, those heading the community are described by the completely secular term *hegoumenoi*, "presidents." They appear as those entrusted with leading the community, which they do in a collegial manner and without being a monarchical head, and they are granted a "position of high authority in the community."[77] They are responsible for preaching the Word (13:7) and as those with the cure of souls they bear responsibility for the salvation of the believers (13:17). But on the other hand no ritual or liturgical functions are ascribed to them.[78] Worship consists of *akoe tou logou*, hearing the Word (2:1; 3:7, 15; 4:2, 7; 5:11). There is no mention of any eucharist. For the author of the letter to the Hebrews neither does it possess a "faith-confirming significance," nor does it herald a substitute for the earlier ritual sacrifice.[79]

But how could so unpriestly a Church become a clerical Church? The factors that led to this were for the most part not derived from the gospel.

---

76. Cf. O. Michel, *Der Brief an die Hebräer*, Göttingen [7]1975, especially pp. 43-50; P.-M. Beaude, in *Dictionnaire de la Bible, Supplément*, X:1318-1334 ("Sacerdoce dans l'épître aux Hébreux").

77. Erich Grässer, "Die Gemeindevorsteher im Hebräerbrief," in Henning Schröer and Gerhard Müller (ed.), *Vom Amt des Laien in Kirche und Theologie. Festschrift für Gerhard Krause*, Berlin 1982, pp. 67-84, here p. 70 (also for what follows).

78. Cf. H.-F. Weiss, *Der Brief an die Hebräer*, Göttingen 1971, p. 712: "A 'hierarchical' structure of Church office is therefore not indicated in this originally secular and frequently used description of office, indeed rather a conscious rejection of a priesthood (mediating Christ's high priesthood) within the Christian community. To the extent that the actual context decides in each case what *hegoumenos* actually means, a hierarchical-priestly character of the office of heading the community is excluded in the letter to the Hebrews."

79. Weiss, *op. cit.*, pp. 724-9, 738-41.

Does the New Testament recognize
a Universal Priesthood
of all Believers?

The real distinction of the laity emphasized in the Council documents is its participation in the universal priesthood, even if this is presented as different in kind from the sacramental priesthood (see p. 23 above).[1] But this inevitably raises the question of the extent to which this doctrine can appeal to the New Testament. Its sole support[2] is the well-known passage in 1 Peter 2:5-10 where the author addresses his audience as follows:

> And like living stones be yourselves built into a spiritual house, to be a holy priesthood, to offer spiritual sacrifices acceptable to God through Jesus Christ. . . . But you are a chosen race, a royal priesthood, a holy nation, God's own people, that you may declare the won-

---

1. With the doctrine of the universal priesthood the Council took up a fundamental concern of the Reformation, though the extent to which it did so deliberately and consciously is an open question. For Luther it was not in any way a question of "merely an anticlerical slogan". For him "the discovery of the universal priesthood, as he understood it, was tied up rather with a new vision of the Church. The 'inner constitution of the Church' was not the hierarchy but 'the universal priesthood of Christians for one another'" (Hans-Martin Barth, *Einander Priester sein. Allgemeines Priestertum in ökumenischer Perspektive*, Göttingen 1990, pp. 29-30). In this the Reformer appealed less to individual passages of scripture such as 1 Pet. 2:5,9 and Rev. 5:10 than to the entire biblical witness (Barth, *op. cit.*, p. 33). Admittedly according to Barth "Luther's ecclesiological insight which crystallized out in his talk of the universal priesthood . . . has only partially reached contemporary Protestantism" (p. 16). This is connected not least with the uncertainty of the terminology: "Universal priesthood . . . must take its bearings from what is meant by 'priesthood'" (p. 18). As we saw (p. 24-25 above), the Second Vatican Council did not make things any easier.

2. The passages from Revelation (1:6, 5:10, and 20:6) continually cited in this context do not carry any weight for our inquiry since for the author of Revelation Christians will "only exercise the sovereign and priestly dignity and power bestowed on them by the redemption when like Christ they have gained

derful deeds of him who called you out of darkness into his marvellous light. Once you were no people but now you are God's people; once you had not received mercy but now you have received mercy.

With the use of several quotations from the Old Testament the whole passage uses a metaphorical language. Those who believe are "living stones" and as such they turn the community into a "spiritual house."[3] Correspondingly the sacrifices offered in this house or community are spiritual sacrifices,[4] and those who offer them are "a holy priesthood." The Temple terminology is preserved but is robbed of its original meaning through its metaphorical application.

This involves a rejection of everything conventionally connected with the Temple and its ritual worship and priesthood. There is no longer any Temple except as an image or metaphor, and the same applies to the priesthood. To deduce from this passage a real priesthood of all believers is to misjudge this metaphorical language.[5] This becomes even more obvious from the

---

victory in death and have resisted the temptation to bow down in worship before the beast and its image. . . . The concept of priest in Revelation is consequently determined neither by the idea of mediation nor by that of sacrifice. Rather it is characterized by the idea of being able to come close to God. So it is understandable that no priestly functions can be predicated of earthly Christians who in baptism are instituted as priests." For a detailed discussion see E. Schüssler Fiorenza, *Priester für Gott. Studien zum Herrschafts- und Priestermotiv in der Apokalypse,* Münster 1972: the quotations come from pp. 419-20.

3. On this image in Qumran and in the New Testament see pp. 49-50 above.

4. See pp. 58-59 above.

5. "The intention of this passage is not in contrast to other concepts of priesthood to ascribe to every baptized person priestly rights and functions, the 'universal priesthood': this intention was read into this passage by the Reformation" (L. Goppelt, *Der erste Petrusbrief,* Göttingen 1978, pp. 145-6). Similarly N. Brox, *Der erste Petrusbrief,* Zürich/Neukirchen[4] 1993, pp. 105-6: "1 Peter applies the phrase *basileion hierateuma* from Ex. 19:6 clearly and unambiguously as a corporative figure for the election, separation and revaluation of a people by God. It applies it as its source [Ex. 19:6] already had done as a unity, as a pleonastic double metaphor for the datum of the special status of the people of God. Exegesis fails to comprehend this meaning if it separates the two terms of the phrase and on top of everything sees itself entitled by the term *hierateuma* to implement an allegorization of various details from ideas about priesthood and apply them to Christians, to their 'dignities,' tasks, and if possible permanent differences or equalizations. Sharing in the priesthood of Christ

continuation in verse 9. The invocation: "You are a chosen race, a royal priesthood, a holy nation, God's own people" is an almost *verbatim* quotation from Exodus 19:5-6: "Now therefore, if you will obey my voice and keep my covenant, you shall be my own possession among all peoples; for all the earth is mine, and you shall be to me a kingdom of priests and a holy nation."

Exodus 19:5-6 provides the most solemn proclamation in the Old Testament of Israel's election, probably deriving from a festive liturgy.[6] This election is described and circumscribed with three concepts:

(a) Israel is Yahweh's own possession. The term *segullah* used here denotes a valuable personal possession. The idea that Israel has become Yahweh's personal possession through his saving act and gracious condescension, in contrast to the other nations, is made clear by the context (v. 4: "You have seen what I did to the Egyptians, and how I bore you on eagles' wings and brought you to myself ").

(b) Election by Yahweh turns Israel into a *mamleket kohanim*, a "kingdom of priests". The entire context, especially the parallel concept "holy nation" that follows, brings out that with the term "priests" the object of reference is not their function but their closeness to God. "The whole of Israel is as it were a priesthood which gathers around Yahweh as its king."[7] We are dealing with a metaphor, and nobody in ancient Israel would have think of deducing a "universal priesthood" of the entire people from this. If this were so, the same or similar statements would be found elsewhere in the Old Testament.

(c) The description of Israel as "a holy nation" (*goy kadosh*) completes the two preceding terms "own possession" and "king-

---

(of which 1 Peter says nothing), the bestowal of this participation in baptism, the equal dignity of all Christians arising from this with the inclusion or exclusion of a special (hierarchical) priesthood—all these in the context of 1 Peter are problems and products of later interpretation, not of this early Christian document itself." So too finally Jürgen Roloff, *Die Kirche im Neuen Testament*, Göttingen 1993, pp. 274-5.

6. On what follows see Hans Wildberger, *Jahwes Eigentumsvolk*, Zürich 1960.

7. Wildberger, *op. cit.*, p. 83.

dom of priests" without adding an additional aspect to them. The person who has access to the realm of God's holiness is "holy." Once again Israel appears as Yahweh's personal possession, rejoicing in his presence and his particular protection.

This proclamation of Israel's status as God's chosen people provided the author of 1 Peter with the ideal scriptural text to offer courage and hope to the "chosen exiles" (1 Pet. 1:1-2) in the diaspora of Asia Minor, troubled by suffering, their faith under attack, oppressed by feelings of faintheartedness and inferiority. In place of the old Israel they now are the chosen people. This is all that the affirmations taken from the proclamation of Israel's chosen status in Exodus 19:5-6 are saying. The individual elements do not have any separate meaning of their own,[8] and to deduce from them a universal priesthood of all believers would be completely erroneous. The New Testament does not recognize any priesthood, whether sacramental or universal.[9]

---

8. Cf. finally J. Ramsay Michaels, *1 Peter* (World Biblical Commentary 49), Waco 1988, pp. 108-9: "The purpose of the phrase 'the King's priesthood' is not so much to characterize the Christian community as specifically priestly in its calling or duties as to complete its identification as 'Israel' against the background of Exodus 19:6."

9. How difficult it is to give the concept "universal priesthood" a content is shown not only by the Council documents but also by the theological literature, for example H. Schlier, "Die neutestamentliche Grundlage des Priesteramtes," in Alfons Deissler and others, *Der priesterliche Dienst. Ursprung und Frühgeschichte*, Freiburg-im-Breisgau 1970, pp. 81-114.

CHAPTER III

From the Community of the Disciples to a Clerical Church

1: Religion without sacrifice under challenge

During the course of the first to the fourth centuries a revolutionary change took place in the way Jesus' followers understood themselves. As is shown by numerous statements in the writings of the New Testament, Jesus' disciples understood themselves quite simply as brothers and sisters, and this not just within a closed community (at the Council of Jerusalem Peter rose to address the brethren, Acts 15:7) but also from community to community (Paul was concerned about "our sister" Phoebe in Rome [Rom. 16:1] and about "our sister" Apphia [Philem. 2]).[1] When they land at Puteoli near Naples Paul and his companions find "brethren" who offer them hospitality (Acts

---

1. In biblical usage the term "brother" means not just the son of the same father or same mother but also covers close relatives, neighbours, friends, colleagues, and members of the same tribe or nation. In the Song of Songs the beloved is addressed as "my sister, my bride." In the Old Testament it is Deuteronomy in particular that emphasizes the brotherhood of all who belong to the nation in contrast to the "stranger" (cf. the rule laid down in Deut. 24:14: "You shall not oppress a hired servant who is poor and needy, whether he is one of your brethren or one of the sojourners who are in your land within your towns"). In the Gospels it is suggestively Matthew above all who by "brother" usually understands a member of one's own community of believers. Things are admittedly different with Jesus, who in open contrast to his own family calls those who do God's will "my brother, and sister, and mother" (Mark 3:31-5, Matt. 12:46-50) and is thus probably looking forward to the beginning of a new human community.

J.-P. Audet, "Priester und Laie in der christlichen Gemeinde," in Alfons Deissler and others, *Der priesterliche Dienst. Ursprung und Frühgeschichte*, Freiburg-im-Breisgau 1970, pp. 115-75, especially pp. 125 ff., demonstrates the development from the original brotherhood to its restriction to clerical brothers in office in the third century, "from a brotherhood with its own initiative and responsibility to a brotherhood canalized in organization and discipline" (p. 150). See also K. H. Schelkle s.v. *Bruder in Reallexikon für Antike und Christentum II*, 635-40.

28:14), and similarly they were welcomed before they had reached the gates of Rome by "brethren" from the community there (Acts 28:15). In 1 Peter 5:9 the Christian community that is already spread over the entire Roman Empire is called the "brotherhood throughout the world." Just the same is found in the *Didache* (see pp. 61–65 above). Those who have just been baptized are introduced into the assembly of those "whom we call brethren" (Justin, *Apol.* 65:1). There may be ministries and offices, but these depend on the community and do not create any distinction of rank.

Things seem quite different in the fourth century. Now there are two classes, the ordained and the non-ordained, clergy and people, *ordo* and *plebs*. There is a hierarchy, a "sacred" government, there are those who give orders and those who obey, there are those who have rights and those who have duties. Above all it is only someone who has been "ordained" who can preside at the eucharist. How could such a departure from the spirit of Jesus have been reached in the Church of Jesus?

In view of the significance the eucharistic meal conducted by community leaders, presidents, elders, prophets, or teachers had (or, as is shown by the letter to the Hebrews, did not have) in early Christian worship, how could the idea that a priest was needed for the celebration of the eucharist emerge? Certainly the very complicated and far from uniform development that led to the ordained episcopate and the ordained priesthood was not determined solely by theological arguments. In certain circumstances an even greater influence was exercised by considerations of politics, canon law, social attitudes, and the struggle for power, and these can only be hinted at here.[2] Of the theological factors at work three in particular need to be mentioned, but without any claim to comprehensiveness:

(1) Suggestions of sacrifice in the accounts of the institution of the eucharist.

---

2. For the influence of the structures of the Roman Empire on the organization of the universal Church see especially Elisabeth Herrmann, *Ecclesia in Re Publica. Die Entwicklung der Kirche von pseudostaatlicher zu staatlich inkorporierter Existenz*, Frankfurt-am-Main/Berne 1980.

(2) The influence of (a) 1 Clement and (b) the dispute with Marcion.

(3) The accusations brought against Christianity by the Roman State because of its lack of ritual.

(1) Suggestions of sacrifice in the accounts of the institution of the eucharist

Let us begin with the accounts of the institution of the eucharist. They have provided grounds for understanding the eucharist as a sacrifice. Talk of "the sacrifice of the Mass" is common among all Catholics. But if there is a sacrifice then there are priests.[3]

As is well known, the story of how the eucharist was established has come down to us in four variants: in the accounts of the Last Supper in Matthew, Mark, and Luke, and in Paul's account in 1 Cor. 11:23-6.[4] This makes it impossible to get back to Jesus' authentic words with any certainty. Rather, contemporary exegesis is unanimous in stating that what we are dealing with here is the aetiology of a form of worship to provide reasons and explanations of the usage of the Christian communities.[5] In other words, what is presented in these accounts is not Jesus' last supper but rather the community's celebratory meal from which the connection was made back to Jesus' last supper (which of course does not mean that the historicity of Jesus' last supper thereby collapses). This echo of Church practice is already evident in the oldest of the Gospels, that according to Mark. Jesus has a meal with his disciples (in Mark, against all histori-

---

3. The eucharist was very early on understood as a commemoration of Jesus' self-sacrifice, as will be shown later. But it is something other to explain the eucharist itself as the performance of a sacrifice (see pp. 101-103 below).

4. This is no place for a full discussion along with references to all the relevant literature. A judicious and comprehensive review has most recently been offered by Thomas Söding ("Das Mahl des Herrn," in B. J. Silberath and D. Sattler (ed.), *Vorgeschmack. Festschrift für Th. Schneider*, Mainz 1995, pp. 134-63), alongside O. Hofius, "Herrenmahl und Herrenmahlsparadosis," in his *Paulusstudien*, Tübingen 1989, pp. 203-40.

5. Helmut Merklein, "Erwägungen zur Überlieferungsgeschichte der neutestamentlichen Abendmahlstraditionen," in *Biblische Zeitschrift* 21 (1977), pp. 88-101, 235-44.

cal probability, it is a passover meal—Mark 14:17 ff.). After a renewed commitment Jesus suddenly speaks over the bread and wine the words that transform their meaning (14:22-5). This doubtless reflects the early Christian custom of the eucharist being preceded or followed by an actual meal.[6]

What is at issue here is the actual course of the Last Supper, or, more precisely, what was actually said over the bread and over the cup. We can start with Mark, even though his version is far from the best, although for what was said over the bread he may well have the best tradition. His text says: "And as they were eating, he took bread, and blessed, and broke it, and gave it to them, and said, 'Take; this is my body'" (Mark 14:22). There is nothing to stop us understanding this as an original saying of Jesus. In it "body" means the person of Jesus, his self, his identity. This saying is all the more striking in that normally at a Jewish meal the bread was distributed silently after the blessing. With these words, which departed from the normal ritual, Jesus assured his disciples of his continuing fellowship with them beyond death. The personal presence that every host offers his guests (see p. 60 above) but which, like all hospitality, is of brief duration, Jesus turned into a constant, lasting presence. This in any case is how the infant Church understood and interpreted what Jesus said and did.

While at a Jewish meal the father of the family is the first to take some of the broken bread,[7] it is not said here that Jesus ate some of the bread himself. Given that he himself is the bread that would not make sense.

On the other hand it is difficult to understand the words said over the cup in Mark as an original parallel to the words said over the bread.[8] They run (Mark 14:23-25): "And he took a cup,

---

6. Willy Rordorf, *Liturgie, foi et vie des premiers chrétiens*, Paris 1986, p. 65 note 2; Eduard Schweizer, *The Good News According to Mark*, Atlanta 1970, London 1971, p. 301: "The juxtaposition of vss. 17-21 and vs. 22 may indicate that it was true also in the Markan church that an entire meal was eaten before bread and wine were served."

7. A variant is that he gives some first to his wife and then takes some for himself.

and when he had given thanks he gave it to them, and they all drank of it. And he said to them, 'This is my blood of the covenant, which is poured out for many. Truly, I say to you, I shall not drink again of the fruit of the vine until that day when I drink it new in the kingdom of God.'"

The first disturbing thing about this is that blood is not a parallel to body but at best to flesh: blood already belongs to the body. Even more striking at first sight is the considerably longer form of the blessing of the cup. What this suggests is that this might be a liturgical re-shaping, similar to the way in which with the Ten Commandments (Ex. 20, Deut. 5) the extended forms of the second, third, fourth, fifth, and tenth commandments are to be ascribed to the liturgical presentation of the decalogue, while the blessing of the bread is set down apodeictically without any reasoned explanation: "Take; this is my body," in a manner similar to the brief imperatives of the first, sixth, seventh, eighth, and ninth commandments.

Admittedly Luke (22:19) already provides a brief explanation: "This is my body, which is given for you"—and Paul provides something analogous but even briefer: "This is my body which is for you" (1 Cor. 11:24). This shows how soon the need was felt for the liturgy not just to perform what Jesus had done but also to interpret it. In the sacramental meal the community is celebrating the death of its Lord, and in doing so it refers to his explicit command to do this in his "remembrance" (Luke 22:19, 1 Cor. 11:24).

The blessing of the cup, however, shows much more strongly the influence of the community liturgy than the blessing of the bread in Luke and Paul (in contrast to Mark and Matthew, where this interpretation is missing), and this in all four versions of the tradition. They are agreed in understanding the Last Supper as the celebration of Jesus' death on the cross in which the new covenant is concluded. So Luke and Paul can formally describe the cup as the covenant: "This cup is the new covenant in my blood" (1 Cor. 11:25), with Luke adding the elucidation:

---

8. This is not to dispute that the Marcan (or pre-Marcan) blessing of the cup could in the history of tradition be older than the Pauline and Lucan variants, cf. Söding, *art. cit.*, pp. 139-46.

"which is poured out for you" (22:20, parallel to "my body, which is given for you"), while Paul repeats the command to do it in his remembrance (1 Cor. 11:25).[9]

What is striking in this is that with Luke and Paul the invitation to drink from the cup is missing, while Mark remembers to report that all (but not Jesus, however) drank from it, and Matthew gives Jesus' formal invitation: "Drink of it, all of you" (26:27).[10] Nor do they give any indication as to the content of the cup, whereas Mark and Matthew describe it as the blood Jesus has shed ("my blood of the covenant" [Mark 14:24], "which is poured out for many" [Matt. 26:28]).[11]

Anyone who is aware that for Jews the consumption of blood was (and still is today) the most horrible imposition will find it difficult to regard a tradition of this kind as original. In the Hellenistic world, "where the indirect consumption of blood, through eating meat that had not been slaughtered in keeping with Jewish law, was something normal, the actual drinking of blood occurred in religious contexts and wine was also recognized as a substitute for blood,"[12] such a formulation could well have been tolerable even for Jewish-Christian ears, even if it would have been unthinkable at first and unlikely to be phrased that way (in conscious or unconscious conformation to the blessing of the bread).

The formula "My blood of the covenant" is thereby also shown to be secondary, in that it is possible only in Greek, but not in Aramaic. In view of the variety of contradictory forms of the

---

9. The liturgy required this repetition as a parallel to the command to do it in his remembrance after the blessing of the bread (Luke 22:19), cf. John Meier, "The eucharist at the Last Supper," in *Theology Digest* 42 (1995), pp. 335-51, here 345: "All argue for the command being an addition by early Christians to make the narrative more clearly a 'cult legend'."

10. "The fact that in Mark the explanation is said after all have drunk may have seemed unsuitable to Matthew. He turns the observation into an imperative: 'Drink of it, all of you' which among other things is parallel to the imperative 'Eat' in v. 26. The dependence on Mark cannot be overlooked" (J. Gnilka, *Das Matthäusevangelium*, part II, Freiburg-im-Breisgau 1988, p. 400).

11. The concern to balance the blessing of the bread is once again due to the liturgy (Meier, *art. cit.*, pp. 345-6).

12. H.-J. Klauck, *Herrenmahl und hellenistischer Kult*, Münster-in-Westfalen ²1986, p. 312.

blessing of the cup, in contrast to the blessing of the bread, the question must be allowed whether the whole tradition with regard to the cup is not the product of the community.[13] The exegete Helmut Merklein, commenting on this, takes the original words that Jesus said over the cup in Mark 14:25 ("I shall not drink again of the fruit of the vine until that day when I drink it new in the kingdom of God"), and comes to this conclusion: "What happened at Jesus' last meal must then be understood as follows. At the end of the meal Jesus took the cup (the cup of blessing), blessed it, and gave it to the disciples to drink. . . . When all had drunk (cf. Mark 14:23b) Jesus said the words recorded in Mark 14:25 and thus gave the meal, which from the start took place under the influence of his death (cf. the blessing of the bread), a character of hope."[14]

The surprising mention of the blood after the blessing of the bread (comprising flesh and blood) could guide our understanding in yet another direction.[15] It is by no means certain that at his last meal Jesus wanted to indicate (within a theology of atonement) his death.[16] Far more natural is the assumption that, in view of the very probable separation that was looming,[17] Jesus wanted simply to impress on his disciples that he would never cease to be there for them. This assurance was advanced by offering the broken bread: "Take, this is me."

But this was not exactly Jesus' last word. If at first it was still possible to forget the end that was threatening, now, just before going out into the night, this possibility too would have to be addressed honestly. What would be more natural than, with the

---

13. Meier, *art. cit.*, p. 341, talks of the "complexity of tradition history in the New Testament".

14. Merklein, "Erwägungen" (note 5 above), pp. 237-8.

15. I am indebted to Meinrad Limbeck for the interpretation of the blessing of the cup that follows.

16. The objections to such an assumption brought by A. Vögtle, "Todesankündigungen und Todesverständnis Jesu," in K. Kertelge (ed.), *Der Tod Jesu*, Freiburg-im-Breisgau 1976, pp. 51-113, have not lost any of their persuasiveness to date.

17. If Jesus' prayer on the Mount of Olives (Mark 14:34-36) is not to be deprived of all seriousness, the arrest and execution threatening Jesus could not yet have been completely unavoidable.

help of the cup full of wine,[18] once again to give the disciples the explicit assurance: "Even if my life is taken away from me by violence,[19] it will not cease to belong to you. I give you my life with this cup. It is my blood for you." ·

This makes understandable that the blessing of the cup in the course of this final meal did not in any way give the disciples the feeling of having really to drink blood. It would also be understandable that the blessing of the cup, once freed from the context of this final meal, was interpreted and presented in such different ways within the framework of celebrations of the Lord's Supper after Easter.

Once again common to all four traditions is the provisional nature of the community meal and its consummation in the eschatological meal at the end of time ("until he comes" [1 Cor. 11:26]; "I shall not drink again of the fruit of the vine until that day when I drink it new in the kingdom of God" [Mark 14:25]). By thereby making both past and future present, the eucharistic meal becomes in the full sense of the word a sacrament, which Thomas Aquinas defines as *commemoratio praeteriti, demonstratio praesentis, et prognosticum futuri*: "a commemoration of the past, a demonstration of the present, and a forecast of the future."[20]

As we have seen, the liturgy increasingly strongly developed the relationship of the eucharist to Jesus' death on the cross. Probably the earliest stage of this understanding is found in Paul, for whom the community, when it "eats this bread and drinks this cup, . . . proclaims the Lord's death until he comes" (1 Cor. 11:26). The death of Jesus, which took place in the past,[21] becomes present for the community in "commemoration."

The Lord present in the meal is the sacrificed paschal lamb, which provides the basis for the community's festival (1 Cor.

---

18. The association of wine and blood was not something new in Israel, cf. Gen 49:11, Deut. 32:14, Isa. 63:2-6, Sir. 39:26, 50:15.

19. It was usual to talk of blood when one was thinking of violent death, cf. Gen. 4:10-11, 9:6, 37:22, Num. 35:33, Deut. 21:7, and other passages.

20. S. Th. III:60:3.

21. For the later inclusion of the resurrection and ascension see Rordorf, "Le sacrifice eucharistique," in *Liturgie, foi et vie des premiers chrétiens*, pp. 73-91, in particular pp. 75-6.

5:7-8). His body is the "body given for you" (Luke 22:19, cf. 1 Cor. 11:24); the cup contains the blood of the covenant poured out "for the forgiveness of sins" (Matt. 26:28). Mention of the blood being poured out and the unmistakable reference to the "blood of the covenant" at the covenant sacrifice on Mount Sinai (Ex. 24:3-8) make it clear how strongly the community was conscious of being included and involved in Jesus' sacrificial action when celebrating the eucharist. It did this in "commemoration," a word that in biblical usage means not just remembering but making present.[22] So Israel had long celebrated the Passover as a "commemoration" (*zikkaron*) of its liberation from alien slavery (Ex. 12:14).[23] Hence the instruction: "In every age everyone is bound to regard himself as if he himself had come out of Egypt."[24]

Joachim Gnilka provides a striking summary of Matthew 26:28: "Participation in the eucharistic meal . . . therefore provides for those taking part personal fellowship with the Christ who suffered, it takes them up into the covenant concluded in his death, and allows them to experience its fruits of salvation, to which belongs in the first place the forgiveness of sins."[25]

In other words, the community makes Jesus' sacrifice its own, his sacrifice of his life becomes its sacrifice. From this it was only a tiny step to understand the eucharist itself as a sacrifice, the point over which the Reformation would split away from the old Church in the sixteenth century. Today we are not that far apart. Nevertheless the relatively early understanding of the eucharist as a sacrifice could not be without significance for the later emergence of a system of priests.

Without a doubt the conviction that God had no need of sacrifices was firmly rooted in early Christianity. Following Jesus'

---

22. Cf. H. Haag, s.v. *Gedächtnis, biblisch in Lexikon für Theologie und Kirche*, Freiburg-im-Breisgau ²1957-67, IV, cols 570-2, and his *Vom alten zum neuen Pascha. Geschichte und Theologie des Osterfestes*, Stuttgart 1971, pp. 115-7.

23. The point is unfortunately obscured by the RSV translation as "a memorial day."

24. Passover Haggadah.

25. J. Gnilka, *Das Matthäusevangelium*, part 2, Freiburg-im-Breisgau 1988, p. 402.

example it radically rejected the bloody sacrifices of the Temple and in doing so had a special liking for making use of the Old Testament texts hostile to ritual (see p. 49 above). The same aversion had also to be directed against all pagan examples of sacrifice, something which, as we shall see, brought Christians into conflict with the Roman State. But this did not stop the infant Church from linking a tangible offering consisting of a material donation with the eucharist right from the start. The writings of the New Testament already suggest that the donation of goods for the poor was a typical element of worship (cf. Acts 4:34-35, 5:1-11, James 2:15-16).[26] In particular for the large-scale collections that Paul organized for the mother Church in Jerusalem (cf. Rom. 15:25-28) the faithful were meant to bring their voluntary contributions along on Sunday, and thus on the occasion of Sunday worship (1 Cor. 16:1-2). Finally, the description of worship given by Justin (see pp. 65-67 above) indicates that the taking up of a collection on behalf of widows and orphans, the sick and those in need, prisoners and strangers, had become a definite part of the celebration of the eucharist.

(2) The Temple as a model in 1 Clement

The first letter of Clement certainly contributed to creating a climate friendly to the idea of a hierarchy. This is a curious document, not only as to what occasioned it and its concept of ministry and community, but also as to its style of argument.[27] Towards the end of the first century a crisis erupted in the Church of Corinth. Some presbyters (elders) were ousted from their ministry and deprived of their liturgical function. In order to eliminate this dispute the community of Rome, without being asked, sent a letter to that of Corinth. While it always uses the first person plural, it is generally linked with the name of the Roman Bishop Clement, who is regarded as its author, even if another minister of the same name is not to be excluded.[28] This

---

26. Rordorf, *op. cit.* (note 21 above), pp. 84-5.

27. Hans von Campenhausen, *Ecclesiastical Authority and Spiritual Power in the Church of the First Three Centuries*, London 1969, pp. 84-95.

28. Andreas Lindemann, *Die Clemensbriefe*, Tübingen 1992, p. 13.

letter acquired such a reputation that in many Churches it was for a long time read out during worship and was even regarded as scripture.

The whole community clearly stood behind the machinations against the presbyters, even if they were instigated by only one or two people (47:6). The affair was all the more reprehensible in that the elders involved could not be charged with any moral lapse or abuse of office. Possibly what was involved was a rebellion of the "young" against the institution of the eldership, which was not yet firmly established in Corinth.[29]

The letter from Rome uses the strongest language to rebuke the Corinth community. The goings-on are described as "the abominable and unholy sedition, alien and foreign to the elect of God, which a few rash and self-willed persons have made to blaze up to such a frenzy that your name, venerable and famous, and worthy as it is of all men's love, has been much slandered" (1:1).[30] What had happened was that "the worthless rose up against those who were in honour, those of no reputation against the renowned, the foolish against the prudent, the young against the old" (3:3).

Although it was a local conflict, it was placed by the author of 1 Clement in a major theological and moral context. In his eyes the old covenant and what had happened in Christ formed a single major order of salvation, and, even if he knew some individual writings of the New Testament,[31] nevertheless for him scripture, the Bible, still remains the Old Testament. "Here it is Christianity which is regarded without question as the revealed religion of the Old Testament. The Christian community is the true

---

29. It is not an argument against this that "jealousy" and "envy" are repeatedly mentioned as the motive (Lindemann, op. cit. p. 16).

30. Quotations from 1 Clement are from the translation by Kirsopp Lake, *The Apostolic Fathers*, vol. 1, Loeb Classical Library, London/Cambridge, Mass., 1912.

31. Certainly 1 Corinthians and Romans, and probably also Hebrews, or at least parts of it.

people of God, and the Bible is exclusively their book."[32] So the author of 1 Clement is incessantly referring back to the Old Testament. He even finds the offices of bishop and deacon established in the Old Testament and proves this with a quotation from Isaiah (60:17) suitably interpreted in this sense (42:5). And to convince the Corinthians that order must reign and that the existing order is willed by God, since he is a God of order, he refers to the order of ritual worship prevailing at the Temple in Jerusalem. There, he says, even though for a long time the Temple itself was no longer extant, "to the High Priest his proper ministrations are allotted, and to the priests the proper place has been appointed, and on Levites their proper services have been imposed. The layman is bound by the ordinances for the laity" (40:5). It is the first time that the concept of the layman appears in Christian writing.[33]

The author of 1 Clement cannot have intended this passage to apply the system prevailing at the Temple literally to the Christian community, but, given the document's level of authority, the reference to the different levels of the hierarchy and the

---

32. von Campenhausen, *The Formation of the Christian Bible*, London 1972, p. 68; cf. Joseph A. Fischer, *Die Apostlischen Väter, griechisch und deutsch*, Darmstadt/Munich 1956, pp. 7-8, 12-13; Lindemann, *op. cit.*, p. 18: "The 'Old Testament' is for the Church of 1 Clement quite simply 'the' holy scripture from which all the instructions necessary for the Christian life are to be taken."

33. Fischer, *op. cit.*, p. 77. This statement is, however, to be used with the greatest care for our contemporary discussion of the laity (cf. chapter 1), the first beginnings of which lie in the third century. In contrast to "the priests" and "the levites," in the plural, the layman (*laikos anthropos*) is referred to in the singular. In this way one group or class (priests, levites) is not being contrasted with another (lay people). Rather the priests and levites serve as a model for those who "have looked into the depths of the divine knowledge" (40:1), something open to all Christians, while the lay person still clings to the (old) people (*laos*) and has not yet pressed forward to the new order of salvation: Jewish Christians who have not yet fully renounced Judaism. In this way we have contrasted with each other those who, in our contemporary parlance, have grasped what being a Christian means (priests and levites as an image or model of this) and those who have not yet grasped this (cf. Alexandre Faivre, *Ordonner la fraternité*, Paris 1992, pp. 171-89: "The layman is the type of the man who thinks he can find his salvation in the ritual worship of the old covenant . . . the man of the unperfected people . . . which does not have access to spiritual knowledge": p. 183).

contrasting position of the laity could not remain without its effect on further development.[34] Even if the contrast between clergy and laity still lies in the distance, this is a first indication of the future devaluation of the laity. A commentator notes that in this concept little more is left to the laity than to belong and to receive the eucharist.[35]

(3) The revaluation of the Old Testament owing to the crisis over Marcion

The acceptance of Old Testament ideas in the Church was further encouraged by the crisis that erupted over the views of Marcion.[36] It was the severest disruption the early Church had experienced, but, like all crises, it had its positive aspects.

Marcion was a well-to-do shipowner from the province of Pontus in Asia Minor: according to a legendary tradition he was the son of the bishop of Sinope, who excommunicated him for seducing a virgin. Around the year 140 Marcion came to Rome. He was accepted by the Christian community and endowed it with considerable funds, but nevertheless he was excluded from it in the year 144. His two major works—his version of the Bible (see below) and his *Antitheses*—have disappeared. They are known of only through polemical writings directed against Marcion and his supporters, especially Irenaeus' *Adversus haereses* of around 180 and Tertullian's *Adversus Marcionem* from about 200. But from these sources it is difficult to determine

---

34. "The purpose of his statement was undoubtedly directed toward calming the unrest in Corinth; to this extent the reference to the Temple system of worship cannot simply be regarded as the norm and foundation of an organization of worship in the Church. But the analogy encouraged the tendency to organize Christian communities according to the model of the old covenant, evidence of which is provided by the difference between the *laikos anthropos* and the holders of office in the Church, to whom belongs the 'offering of the gifts' (44:4)" (Peter Stockmeier, *Glaube und Religion in der frühen Kirche*, Freiburg-im-Breisgau 1973, pp. 66-7).

35. R. Knopf, *Die Apostolischen Väter*, vol. I, Tübingen 1920, p. 114.

36. On Marcion, the most up-to-date summary is to be found in B. Aland, *Theologische Realenzyklopädie*, vol. 22, 1992, pp. 89-101 (with references to the literature). The standard authoritative work remains Adolf von Harnack's pioneering study, *Marcion: Das Evangelium vom fremden Gott*, Leipzig ²1924, reprinted Darmstadt 1996.

with certainty what comes from Marcion himself, what from his interpreters, the "Marcionites," and what their opponents have made of all this. Nevertheless, no doubt is possible about Marcion's essential theses. His teaching spread quickly, led to the foundation of numerous churches, and during persecution proved its worth with a crop of martyrs. At the beginning of the third century Tertullian states that Marcion's teaching has filled the whole world.

In Marcion's view there are unbridgeable differences ("antitheses") between the Old and New Testaments. The Father of Jesus Christ proclaimed by the New Testament is, he says, someone other than the God of the Old Testament. The latter in his view is a capricious, ignorant, cruel, biased, and despotic deity, whereas Jesus preached mercy and peace. And in any case the prophecies of the Old Testament announced a different Messiah than him who appeared in Jesus Christ.

So Marcion rejected the Old Testament in its entirety. There was thus no room for it in the Christian Church. But because the Old Testament Judaic way of thinking was also reflected in the New Testament alongside the pure teaching of Jesus, Marcion created for himself his own New Testament consisting only of the Gospel according to Luke (suitably bowdlerized according to Marcion's ideas) and ten Pauline epistles.

The fact that for a hundred years the Old Testament had not been questioned and had been without dispute the Church's Bible indicates the upheaval Marcion must have meant for the Church of the second century. "She had lost her 'scriptures'; at one and the same moment her proud claims to be the religion of the most ancient wisdom and the religion of historical fulfilment were both rendered invalid. The 'archives' from which for so long she had confidently drawn the highest knowledge, and had refuted and convinced both Jew and heathen, were now to be burnt. The one sacred document of the Christian revelation was apparently the work of a different God; the foundation on which Christians had believed themselves to stand had sunk into the abyss."[37]

---

37. von Campenhausen, *The Formation of the Christian Bible*, p. 178.

In the meantime, of course, there was a New Testament. By the middle of the second century this was available in its entirety. So sooner or later the question unavoidably arose whether the Church should stick with the old Bible and supplement it with the new, as if with a final chapter—or should the new Bible replace the old? Marcion's achievement was to have stimulated and hastened this decision. The Church opted for the second choice: the Old and New Testaments together formed the Christian Bible.

As a result the Old Testament now acquired a completely new status in the Church. If previously it had been the Jewish Bible that the Church had appropriated for itself and interpreted in the light of Christ, it was henceforth the Christian Bible. The Old Testament was transformed from a Jewish into a Christian book.[38] Not surprisingly, its institutions, including ritual worship and priesthood, acquired a new weight as a result.

(4) The Roman State as champion of sacrificial worship

In the end it was also the persecution of the infant Church by the Roman State that decisively encouraged the element of ritual worship to gain the upper hand.[39] Christianity was spreading in a state that was pagan but in no way godless. The environment in which the message of Jesus was proclaimed was to a considerable extent shot through with religious ideas. The difficulty the Jews had already had in accepting the rejection of the Temple and its worship by the Jesus community is shown by Stephen's speech and his being lynched (Acts 7). But even in pagan attacks the religious element occupied an important place. According to Tacitus,[40] the Christian faith counted as *exitiabilis superstitio*, "a pernicious superstition." From the second century BC onward the term *superstitio* had taken on the derogatory con-

---

38. K. Beyschlag, *Grundriß der Dogmengeschichte*, vol. I, Darmstadt 1982, p. 77.

39. For what follows see above all Peter Stockmeier, "Christlicher Glaube und antike Religiosität," in H. Temporini and W. Haase, *Aufstieg und Niedergang der römischen Welt*, Berlin 1972, pp. 871-909.

40. Annals XV:44:3; Peter Guyot and Richard Klein, *Das frühe Christentum bis zum Ende der Verfolgungen*, Darmstadt 1993-4, vol. 1, pp. 16-17.

notation of an unreasonable religious belief, or superstition in the current sense,[41] in contrast to *religio*. If *religio* comprised the strict due observance of the ritual worship, *superstitio* was a false relationship to the gods. Ultimately, a religion's relationship to ritual worship decided whether it corresponded to the requirements of the Roman State or not.

So it is not surprising to find that Christians were accused of atheism, of godlessness. Tertullian makes clear what was meant by this. The complaint brought against the Christians was "Deos non colitis," "You do not honour the gods, and you do not offer any sacrifice for the emperor."[42] This accusation was devastating in the light of the fact that the Roman people were convinced that the decline of traditional religion would result in the decline of the empire. It is not hard to imagine how difficult it must have been for Christians to hold their own with their modest meals against the pomp of the Roman ritual of sacrifice. For this reason they were concerned to expose this sacrificial ritual to ridicule and, in the sense of the prophets and of Jesus, to expound the idea that true worship is that of the heart and of love. Justin Martyr (see pp. 65-67 above) puts this objection to the pagans:

> But nor do we honour with many sacrifices and garlands of flowers those whom men have sculpted and set up in temples and called gods, since we recognize that these are lifeless and dead and do not have the form of God. . . . But we have also received the teaching that God does not need any material offering from men, since we see that he provides everything.   We have been taught and have been persuaded and believe that he accepts only those who imitate the good that belongs to him, temperance and justice and benevolence and whatever is proper to God.[43]

---

41. Originally it was neutral and meant being affected by the divine or that which came from the gods, "anxious fear in the face of what transcended the human dimension" (Stockmeier, *art. cit.* p. 888), cf. the entry in *Der kleine Pauly*, vol. V, 1975.

42. *Apology* 10:1; Guyot and Klein, *op. cit.* vol. 2, pp. 140-1.

43. *Apology* 9-10.

A similar argument comes from the Roman apologist Minucius Felix (around 200 AD). Against his pagan interlocutor Caecilius, who argues for retaining the traditional worship of the gods since this has made Rome great, he presents the counter-argument:

> Do you think we hide what we worship, if we have no shrines or altars? What image should I shape of God when, if you are right, man himself is the image of God? What temple should I build for him when the whole of this world that was made by his labour cannot comprehend him? . . . Should he not better be consecrated in our minds, hallowed in the depths of our hearts? Should I offer God sacrifices and victims which he has produced for my benefit and throw his gifts back at him? This is ingratitude, when a fit sacrifice is a good disposition and a pure mind and a clear conscience. Therefore anyone who cultivates innocence prays to God, anyone who cultivates justice makes an offering to God, anyone who abstains from deceit propitiates God, anyone who snatches someone from danger sacrifices the best victim. These are our sacrifices, these are the holy things of God.[44]

Finally, the Christian philosopher Athenagoras, round about the year 177, sent the emperor Marcus Aurelius and his son Commodus a petition on behalf of the Christians. In it he explains:

> Since the majority of those accusing us of atheism, though they have not even the foggiest notion of the nature of God, are ignorant of scientific or theological doctrine and have no acquaintance with them, and measure piety in terms of sacrifices; since they accuse us of not recognizing the same gods as do the cities, I ask you to take the following into account, my sovereigns, in dealing with both issues. First, concerning our refusal to sacrifice, the Artificer and Father of this universe needs no blood, fat, or the fragrance of flowers and incense. He himself is the perfect fragrance and is in need of nothing from within or without. . . . So then, when . . . we raise up holy hands to him [God], what further need does he have of any hecatomb?[45]

---

44. *Octavius* 32.

45. Athenagoras, *Legatio and de Resurrectione*, edited and translated by William R. Schroedel, Oxford 1972, §13, pp. 27-8.

At the same time efforts were being made to ascribe a sacrificial character to the simple eucharistic meal.[46] As we have seen (cf. p. 67 above), the understanding of the eucharist as sacrifice begins to emerge as early as Justin. Admittedly he is definite in regarding the eucharist as a commemoration and realization of the passion of Jesus. Nevertheless the distinction between *memoria* (commemoration) and sacrifice seems to become blurred with him. This is suggested above all by his frequent reference to the promise in Malachi (1:10-12) of a pure offering in every place and its fulfilment in the eucharist.[47] "He prophesies about the sacrifices offered to him in every place by us the nations, that is the bread of the eucharist and likewise the cup of the eucharist."[48]

Nevertheless in the whole of Christian literature of the first two centuries the term *hiereus, sacerdos,* "priest," is avoided. This was to change during the third century.

2: Hierarchy in development

(1) Community and ministry in the epistles of the New Testament

This development took place in a variety of ways and has been described by extremely competent authors.[49] The idea of some kind of "superior authority" was alien to the early Christian com-

---

46. Stockmeier, *art. cit.,* p. 899.

47. Charles Munier, *L'Apologie de Saint Justin Philosophe et Martyr,* Fribourg 1994, p. 139.

48. *Dialogue with Trypho* XLI:3.

49. For the first three centuries in particular see von Campenhausen, *Ecclesiastical Authority and Spiritual Power in the Church of the First Three Centuries,* and "Die Anfänge des Priesterbegriffs in der alten Kirche," in his *Tradition und Leben,* Tübingen 1960, pp. 272-89; Alexandre Faivre, *Naissance d'une hiérarchie,* Paris 1977, *Les laïcs aux origines de l'Eglise,* Paris 1984, and *Ordonner la fraternité.* For the New Testament period see Wilhelm Pesch, "Priestertum und Neues Testament," in Pesch and others, *Priestertum—Kirchliches Amt zwischen gestern und morgen,* Aschaffenburg 1971, pp. 10-35; Reinhard M. Hübner, "Die Anfänge von Diakonat, Presbyterat und Episkopat in der frühen Kirche," in Albert Rauch and Paul Imhof (ed.), *Das Priestertum in der Einen Kirche. Diakonat, Presbyterat und Episkopat,* Aschaffenburg 1987, pp. 45-89; Karl Kertelge, *Gemeinde und Amt im Neuen Testament,* Munich 1972; Paul

munities. Admittedly Paul does not hesitate to bring secondary debates to an end with an authoritative pronouncement (1 Cor. 11:16).[50] And he did not shrink from putting himself as an example worthy of imitation before the eyes of his "beloved children" whom he had begotten "through the gospel" (1 Cor. 4:14-16, cf. 11:1, Phil. 4:9, Philemon 10), indeed in the worst case even from threatening them with "a rod" (1 Cor. 4:21).[51] But as soon as it was a question of the individual community making its solidarity with Christ a reality, then for Paul the community as a whole, which means the entire body of Christ,[52] was obliged to joint action, but not to silent obedience: for example with the

---

Hoffmann, "Priestertum und Amt im Neuen Testament," in Hoffmann (ed.), *Priesterkirche*, Düsseldorf ²1989, pp. 12-61. For the fundamental issue cf. H. Ritt, who following Roloff warns against any premature systematization of offices and ministries in the New Testament: "The situation with regard to the sources does not allow us to trace unambiguous lines of development" ("Priestersein heißt: 'Von Gottes maßloser Liebe Zeugnis geben'," in J. Schreiner (ed.), *Freude am Gottesdienst. Festschrift für J. G. Plöger*, Stuttgart 1983, pp. 383-93, here 390). For office and ministry as a whole (with references to the literature) see W. Beinert, "Autorität um der Liebe willen. Zur Theologie des kirchlichen Amtes," in K. Hillenbrand (ed.), *Priester heute*, Würzburg 1990, pp. 32-66.

50. For the problem addressed in 1 Cor. 11:2-16, the solution of which "remains below the proper Pauline level and is to be gauged by Gal. 3:28," cf. most recently W. Schrage, *Der erste Brief an die Korinther*, vol. 2, Düsseldorf/ Neukirchen 1995, pp. 487-541, 525.

51. Cf. on this Klaus Schäfer, *Gemeinde als "Bruderschaft." Ein Beitrag zum Kirchenverständnis des Paulus*, Berne 1989, pp. 353-69, 657-67. He characterizes Paul's image of himself as father "paradoxically" as "brotherly fatherliness" but also finds integrated in it "strongly feminine and maternal traits such as tenderness and warmheartedness" (cf. 1 Thess. 2:7 ff., Gal 4:19-20, 2 Cor. 6:11-13, 7:22-23), in sharp contrast to the pastoral epistles. "There the community is presented as the 'house of God' over which the office-bearers 'preside' as the father or administrator of the household in an authoritative and patriarchal way, completely analogous to the ancient world's ideas of the *paterfamilias*. This structuring of the community in the categories of above and below, giving orders and obeying, educating and listening, teaching and learning, with a clear division of roles, is not to be found in Paul" (pp.. 368-9).

52. The deuteropauline epistles are the first to think of the universal Church when reference is made to the "body of Christ," cf. J. Hainz, "Vom 'Volk Gottes' zum 'Leib Christi'," in *Jahrbuch für Biblische Theologie 7* (1992), pp. 145-64; Jürgen Roloff, *Die Kirche im Neuen Testament*, Göttingen 1993, pp. 96-9.

celebration of the Lord's Supper (1 Cor. 11:17-34),[53] but also for questions of discipline (1 Cor. 5:1-13).[54] So Paul takes it completely for granted that alongside apostles (and not subordinate to them) prophets and teachers should also exercise their ministries (1 Cor. 12:28, cf. Eph. 4:11). Indeed, prophets and teachers already played a decisive role in the community of Antioch (Acts 13:1),[55] and, as we have seen (see p. 65 above), in the community reflected in the *Didache* the bishops and deacons have difficulty in making headway over against the prophets and teachers. But in the Pauline communities there are yet others who contribute their gifts for the benefit of the community, gifts that are the fruit of the Spirit, such as healing, giving advice, comforting, and providing practical help (Rom. 12, 1 Cor. 12). All the baptized "should take seriously the fact that every member of the body of Christ has a particular dignity and is called to share responsibility in building up a community of brothers and sisters under the guidance of the Holy Spirit; privilege and discrimination must from now on be excluded, since the various charisms and 'offices' do not provide the basis for any domination in the community, but rather they are ultimately administered and controlled by the entire community and furthermore understood as ministry (*diakonia*) for the Lord and the brethren."[56] So the end of the first century provides a somewhat surprising enumeration of the "gifts " of Christ in the letter to the Ephesians: apostles, prophets, evangelists, pastors, and teachers (4:11). The

53. Cf. Hoffmann, *art. cit.*, p. 29: "In 1 Cor. 11 its execution appears as the affair of the entire community." Similarly H.-J. Klauck, 1. *Korintherbrief*, Würzburg 1984, p. 82: "It is notable that Paul does not address any single individual directly and make him responsible for the proper conduct of affairs, which he would almost certainly have had to do if there had been only a single community leader."

54. The apostle cannot simply anticipate the verdict of the community (1 Cor. 5:4-5, 13; 2 Cor. 6-8). Cf. in detail most recently W. Schrage, *Der erste Brief an die Korinther*, vol. I, Zürich/Neukirchen 1991, pp. 367-85.

55. It must have been from Antioch that Paul took over the triad apostle (in its original meaning of someone sent out, an envoy, cf. Acts 14:4, 14), prophet, teacher: cf. Merklein, *Das kirchliche Amt nach dem Epheserbrief*, Munich 1973, pp. 249-60, Alfred F. Zimmermann, *Die urchristlichen Lehrer*, Tübingen 1984, pp. 92-135.

56. Schäfer, *op. cit.*, p. 407.

survey encompasses both past and present. The mention of "pastors" shows that meanwhile "a central role has accrued to the leaders of the community."[57]

The more clearly it became apparent that the age of the apostles was reaching its end, the greater the pressure, almost inevitably,[58] for a permanent structure of office and ministry. It is presumably the beginnings of such a development that we find in one of the later Pauline epistles, that to the Philippians, where there is for the first time mention of "overseers" (*episkopoi*) and "servants" (*diakonoi*), even if they are only mentioned after "the saints," the believers (1:1). But there is no question of these *episkopoi* and *diakonoi* exercising sacred offices or ministries, or indeed forming a hierarchy, a priestly order.[59] Nor did the

---

57. Hoffmann, *art. cit.*, p. 35. How the leaders of the community came to be described as "pastors" without "Christological mediation," i.e. without recourse to Christ's pastoral office, is made clear by Merklein, *op. cit.* pp. 372-92.

58. But only *almost* inevitably. The Johannine community indicates that it is not simply the gospel that produces a ministerial structure in the community of Jesus' disciples; cf. H.-J. Klauck, *Gemeinde—Amt—Sakrament*, Würzburg 1989, p. 218: "Were there offices and office-holders in the Johannine community? This is not least a question of definition. If we choose the ideas of office in the pastoral epistles and in Ignatius of Antioch as the basis for comparison, we shall have to reply that this kind of office was for a long time unknown to the Johannine community and one which, when the community got to know it in whatever form, it did not at first accept for itself. A community structured in terms of offices was something that people only came to terms with on attaching themselves, under the pressure of events, to the Petrine Church and becoming permanently involved with the universal Church."

59. The term *episkopos* is of totally secular origin and comes from the sphere of administration and service. "The *episkopoi* of the epistle to the Philippians were however certainly not just functionaries for the administration of the community who were responsible for looking after its finances. Rather the charisms of helping and administrating mentioned in 1 Cor. 12:28 have found in them their personal institutionalization. The area of the community's activities that was most in need of help and administration was worship. Here one could not cope permanently on a basis of improvization: consistency and a settled structure were necessary. The various house-communities needed permanent meeting-places and some control or regulation of presiding at the eucharist. In addition it was necessary to co-ordinate the various house-communities. So the supposition that the *episkopoi* in Philippi were the presidents of that city's house-communities seems the most likely. It was thus a question of a local office of leadership with a spiritual aspect" (Jürgen Roloff, *Die Kirche im Neuen Testament*, Göttingen 1993, p. 142).

"elders" (*presbuteroi*) who looked after the destiny of the local Church in Jewish Christian communities (in Jerusalem, Acts 11:30, 15:2, 4, 6; in Ephesus, Acts 20:17).[60] These elders—who were also, at least to begin with, older men—preserved in an ideal way the continuity of the post-apostolic local Church with the founding generation in the Pauline and Johannine communities.[61] Common to both structures is the fact that the office of leadership draws to itself the functions relevant for the communities, "especially those of teaching and leading worship."[62]

It was, however, inevitable that the two patterns (*episkopoi* and *diakonoi* on the one hand and *presbuteroi* on the other) should mingle, so that in the epistle to Titus (1:5-7) the language switches from "elders" to the qualities required of a bishop (*episkopos*).

This indicates that the author's intention was to equate elders, whose presence he had to reckon with in at least some of the communities he was addressing, with *episkopoi*, so as to interpret the office of elder on the basis of the office of *episkopos*. Involved in this is not just the replacement of one concept by another. The structure of elders, going back to Jewish models, rested on the principle of the respect naturally granted to age, experience, and social status. The office of elder was an honorary office with sharply representative characteristics. Members of the college of elders were the members of the community who

60. Roloff, *op. cit.*, p. 81: "The system of elders was suggested by the Jewish world, where it served to develop certain established forms of structuring the community. In the synagogue the elder was the representative of tradition who handed on his experience of the Law and thus helped to maintain the continuity of the life of the community. The qualification for this was maturity and a worthy life. Hence as a rule it was men of advanced age who were chosen for the post. In the primitive Christian community it could hardly have been different. It was reliable, tried and tested Christians who as a committee had to decide on certain questions affecting the life of the community and who as individuals provided what help was needed and undertook administrative tasks. In any case the elders represent an element of an ordered structure."

61. Hoffmann, *art. cit.*, pp. 38-39; possibly that is why Polycarp (around the year 135) finds presbyters in Philippi instead of the *episkopoi* mentioned by Paul (Polycarp 6:1-2. 11:1). For elders in the Johannine community (2 John 1, 3 John 1) cf. Klauck, *op. cit.*, p. 207.

62. Hoffmann, *art. cit.*, p. 32.

were publicly respected. But this contradicted the reliance on charisms or gifts, since in the Pauline communities actual ministries emerged through charisms being recognized and particular competences and gifts being put to use for building up the Church (1 Cor. 12:28-31). It was precisely on this basis that the office of *episkopos* rested: it is defined by a particular task, and as a result it presupposes particular competences and gifts. By favouring it the pastoral epistles show themselves to be fundamentally bound to the Pauline reliance on charisms. In actuality they seem to have conceived of the transition from a structure based on elders to one based on *episkopoi* in such a way that at one stage one member of a community's council of elders emerged who in a special way took over responsibility for preaching and leading the community and thus was qualified for *episkope* (1 Tim. 5:17). The tacit presupposition in this is that in each community there should be only one episkopos as the responsible leader. This arises from understanding the community as an extended family which could have only one *paterfamilias* or head of the household. A development that necessarily leads to the monoepiscopate is thus set on its way.[63]

Correspondingly Paul as reported by Luke exhorts the presbyters of Ephesus in his farewell speech in Miletus (Acts 20:28): "Take heed to yourselves and to all the flock, in which the Holy Spirit has made you guardians (*episkopous*), to feed the Church of the Lord."[64]

The structure of elders also necessarily involved office in the Church becoming something for men only, while among the deacons there were without a doubt women too (1 Tim. 3:11),[65] and

---

63. Roloff, *op. cit.*, pp. 261-2. For more detail see his *Der erste Brief an Timotheus*, Zürich/Neukirchen 1988, pp. 169-89.

64. Luke too is therefore trying to reshape the old Palestinian structure of elders by linking it with the (Pauline) structure of *episkopoi* and *diakonoi*; cf. Roloff, *op. cit.*, pp. 220-1 and 262 note 26. Correspondingly *episkopos* is to be understood here as denoting a function and not an office (as also 1 Clement 42:4-5; Fischer, *op. cit.*, p. 10, says anachronistically "bishops, not simple priests").

65. "Everything favours the conclusion that verse 11 denotes not deacon's wives but women deacons, and thus office-holders" (G. Lohfink, "Weibliche Diakone im Neuen Testament," in G. Dautzenberg (ed.), *Die Frau im Urchristentum*, Freiburg-im-Breisgau 1983, ²1992, pp. 320-338, here 333). J.

indeed slave women,[66] while the *diakonos* Phoebe, in whose house the community of Cenchreae clearly gathered (Rom. 16:1-2), would also have presided at the eucharist. The same applies to Prisca and Aquila and "the church in their house" (Rom. 16:3-5), to Andronicus and Junia or Julia who were reckoned among the apostles (Rom. 16:7), and to "Nympha and the church in her house" (Col. 4:15).[67] On the other hand it is striking that in the pastoral epistles (1 and 2 Timothy, Titus)[68] no liturgical function is ascribed to bishop and presbyters (there is no hierarchical difference of rank between them). Rather there "for the first

---

D. Davies, "Deacons, Deaconesses and the Minor Orders in the Patristic Period" (in *The Journal of Ecclesiastical History* 14 [1963], pp. 1-150, argues firmly against this understanding and proves that the office of women deacons arose in the Eastern Church in the first half of the third century and in the Western Church not before the fifth century. In any case one must beware of drawing a direct line from possible women deacons in the New Testament to the much later Church office of deaconesses, whose task it was to visit women who were ill and bring them the eucharist and also to help with the baptism of women, but without being able to play a part in the liturgy and, like male deacons, act in the place of the presbyter in his absence.

66. The younger Pliny reports from the dual province of Bithynia and Pontus in his letter to the emperor Trajan (Ep. X:96, written between 111 and 113) that he had had two women slaves tortured "who were called deacons" (*quae ministrae dicebantur*). "The statement about the two *ministrae* ('deaconesses') is the earliest evidence that slaves could occupy inferior offices in the community" (Guyot and Klein, *op. cit.* vol. 1, pp. 38-41). The same reservations about this interpretation ("deaconesses") are to be found in Davies, *art. cit.* In actual fact it is remarkable that for a hundred and fifty years after this we hear no more of deaconesses.

67. Both Junia/Julia and Nympha, who were still women in the fourth century Vulgate, were turned into men by a later tradition (for the details cf. besides the commentaries on these passages also H.-J. Klauck, "Vom Reden und Schweigen der Frauen in der Urkirche," in his *Gemeinde—Amt—Sakrament*, pp. 232-45). For the house churches of Roman cities in the first and second centuries and the rooms they used for worship see Peter Lampe, *Die stadtrömischen Christen in den ersten beiden Jahrhunderten*, Tübingen 1987, especially pp. 307-20. (An English translation is in preparation for publication in 1999—Trans.) During the first two centuries there were no "house churches" in the sense of rooms specially set apart for worship in private houses. "The Christians of the first and second centuries celebrated their services in rooms which in normal daily life were used by the inhabitants for other purposes" (p. 309).

68. "Later than the first third of the second century", Hübner, *art. cit.* (n. 49 above), p. 64.

time the office is treated as essentially and comprehensively a teaching office."[69] A similar situation is found in the epistle of James (end of the first century). The presbyters form what one could almost call an incidental element, good for visiting the sick and praying over them (James 5:14).[70] Those who set the tone are rather the teachers.[71]

While the Shepherd of Hermas[72] is definitely not yet aware of a monarchical episcopate, different judgments are made as to

---

69. von Campenhausen, *Ecclesiastical Authority and Spiritual Power in the Church of the First Three Centuries*, p. 109; cf. also Roloff, *op. cit.*, p. 263: "It is the competence to teach of the *episkopos* that is cited as his single specifically spiritual characteristic: a first indication that for the pastoral epistles the office of leading the community is a teaching office."

70. Maliciously: they can thereby at least do no harm.

71. Cf. J. Wanke, "Die urchristlichen Lehrer nach dem Zeugnis des Jakobusbriefes," in R. Schnackenburg and others, *Die Kirche des Anfangs. Festschrift für H. Schürmann*, Leipzig 1977, pp. 489-511; Zimmermann, *op. cit.* (n. 55 above), pp. 194-208; on teachers in general, besides Zimmermann, see especially H. Schürmann, "... und Lehrer," in *Dienst der Vermittlung. Festschrift zum 25jährigen Bestehen des Philosophisch-Theologischen Studiums im Priesterseminar Erfurt*, Leipzig 1977, pp. 107-47. For the second century, following on from Zimmermann, see the comprehensive monograph by Ulrich Neymeyr, *Die christlichen Lehrer im zweiten Jahrhundert*, Leiden 1989. Points worth bringing out include: "The sources do not answer the question where these Christian teachers obtained their living expenses from if they neither enjoyed significant family wealth nor exercised their teaching activity alongside their proper calling. . . . Probably Christian teachers did not demand any fees of their pupils or audience. But on the basis of the wide spread of patronage in the educational system of the ancient world it is entirely conceivable that Christian teachers too were supported by wealthy Christian patrons, as Eusebius reports of Origen. Less probable, on the other hand, is the likelihood that the Christian teachers who are the object of this study were paid by the Christian communities or congregations, since nothing indicates that they did their teaching at the behest of the community, and they were not office-holders. But neither of these exclude the possibility that the Christian teachers of the second and early third centuries were in active contact with the Christian communities or congregations: indeed their relationship to the community can rather generally be demonstrated. . . . Christian teachers of this type existed until the middle of the third century. Afterwards teachers who were not clerics became the exception. . . . From the middle of the third century onwards the function of Christian teachers was taken over by the *episkopoi* and presbyters" (pp. 235-8).

72. A penitential tract written in Rome around the year 140 by a respected Christian named Hermas, which was regarded as canonical by many Fathers.

whether the pastoral epistles show the community already being led by a single bishop[73] and whether Polycarp is the monarchical bishop of Smyrna.

More important for our subject, however, than the question of particular offices and ministries is the fact that in the pastoral epistles there is already a certain distance between office-holders and the community. "Responsibility has been transferred to the office-holders alone. . .: the community is exclusively the opposite number of the office-holder and the object of his pastoral concern. . . . It is [at worship] a praying and listening community," which no longer has any involvement in the selection and appointment of the office-holder.[74]

(2) Ignatius of Antioch

A decisive turning-point in this development is shown by the letters of the bishop and martyr Ignatius of Antioch, which recent research dates to between the years 160 and 170.[75] He provides the earliest evidence for the monarchical episcopate and the hierarchy of bishop (always in the singular), presbyterium, and deacons. This seems now to be the prevailing Church order. As bishop of Antioch Ignatius is not alone. Rather, according to his description, bishops have already been appointed "throughout the world" (Eph. 3:2). "Do nothing without" (or "apart from") the bishop" is his motto. The bishop represents Christ. Hence the believers should be subject to the bishop as to Christ (Trall. 2:1). "It is good to know God and the bishop. He who honours the bishop has been honoured by God; he who does anything without the knowledge of the bishop is serving the devil" (Smyrn. 9:1). Ignatius deplores the fact that "there are some who recognize the bishop in their words, but disregard him in all their actions. Such men seem to me not to act in good faith" (Magn. 4).

---

73. This view is upheld especially by von Campenhausen, *op. cit.*, pp. 107–8, while it is rejected by N. Brox, *Die Pastoralbriefe*, Regensburg 1969, p. 43: "We cannot yet speak of the monarchical episcopate." Hübner (*art. cit.*, pp. 65–6) takes a similar view.

74. Brox, *op. cit.*, pp. 46 and 44; cf. Hübner, *art. cit.*, p. 68.

75. Hübner, *art. cit.*, p. 78. The quotations are from the translation by Kirsopp Lake, *Apostolic Fathers*, vol. 1.

The bishop, however, does not exist on his own, but only linked with the presbyters and deacons. To honour these and subordinate oneself to them is just as much a duty as it is with regard to the bishop. "As then the Lord was united to the Father and did nothing without him . . ., so do you do nothing without the bishop and the presbyters" (Magn. 7:1). Anyone who does anything apart from the bishop, presbyters and deacons is "outside the sanctuary" (Trall. 7:2).

In this tripartite order of bishop, presbyter and deacon the clergy as a class and the hierarchy unmistakably become apparent. And now the circle closes. It was the eucharist that stimulated the unique status of the bishop.[76] Bishop and eucharist fuse into a single unity. He is the guarantee of the unity that is represented and brought about by the eucharist. "Be careful therefore to use one eucharist, for there is one flesh of our Lord Jesus Christ, and one cup for union with his blood, one altar (*thusiasterion*), as there is one bishop with the presbytery and the deacons" (Philad. 4). If it is demanded that only the eucharist that takes place under the presidency of the bishop or someone commissioned by him should count as reliable (Smyrn. 8:1), then what is being appealed to is the authority of the bishop and not some ordination that singles him out. The faithful stand over against the hierarchy of bishop, presbyters, and deacons, but not yet as a class of laity over against a class of clergy. Those who hold office are not "clerics."[77]

That change took place at the beginning of the third century, almost as it were overnight (just as throughout history there have always been revolutions that have taken place overnight simply because the time was ripe for them). Admittedly nothing of this can yet be gleaned from Irenaeus of Lyons (around the year 200). As von Campenhausen emphasizes, the latter "does not contemplate a special sacramental 'character' of the episcopate, nor does he ever stress the authority of the bishops as opposed to that of the laity, or indeed to that of the other non-episcopal clergy of

---

76. Fischer, *Die Apostolischen Väter, griechisch und deutsch*, p. 127.

77. Christ, whom the bishop represents, is only once referred to as high priest (*archiereus*) (Philad. 9:1).

the Church."[78] Nevertheless the development into a two-tier Church consisting of ordo and plebs, clergy and laity, could not be delayed, as Tertullian testifies for the Church of Carthage, Hippolytus for Rome, and Clement and Origen for Alexandria.[79]

(3) The Church becomes a clerical Church

During the course of the third century the separation between clergy and laity became a *fait accompli*. The Church became a clerical Church. On the one side was the presbyterium presided over by the bishop (who at one moment belongs to it and at the next stands above it), on the other the faithful.[80]

Already in the first quarter of the third century Hippolytus presents us in the *Apostolic Tradition* (whether it is genuinely the work of Hippolytus or not is irrelevant) with a more or less clear Church order: the bishop is the high priest, shepherd, teacher, and the person who makes the decisions for the community. He is surrounded by the presbyterium. Bishop, presbyters, and deacons form the clergy (*ordo, clerus, proedria*).[81] What divides the clergy as a whole from the laity is the conduct of worship. There are other classes of ministers,[82] but these were merely appointed to their posts. The clergy, on the other hand, were ordained by the laying on of hands, because they played a role in the liturgy. This demanded an act of dedication or consecration. However, this act of dedication should not be equated with ordination to the priesthood as it became established from the fifth century onward. It is not an ordination *ad personam*, which adheres to the recipient but, we could say, an ordination *ad officium*, which enables someone to fulfil an office. It exists

---

78. von Campenhausen, *op. cit.*, p. 172. On the question of sacramental character he adds in a footnote: "Such a concept does not seem to be entertained by any writer of this period."

79. Faivre, *Les laïcs aux origines de l'Eglise*, pp. 95-7.

80. Albano Vilela, *La condition collégiale des prêtres au IIIe siècle*, Paris 1971, p. 387.

81. The term *ordo* includes the widows, whereas only men belong to the *clerus*.

82. Subdeacons, acolytes, exorcists, lectors, porters, widows. The subdeacons were the deacons' assistants. One reason for their existence was that the number of deacons remained as a rule restricted to seven, with reference to Acts 6:5.

only as long as the office does. It is strictly conditioned by and linked to the office. It is not a sacrament but the conferment of an office.[83]

(4) Sacrifice, therefore priest

It is no accident that the institution of the priesthood emerges with the start of the third century. "The word *sacerdos*, 'priest', appears for the first time for Christian bishops and also presbyters in Tertullian."[84] The reason is that the understanding of the eucharist as sacrifice is also firmly established from the start of the third century onward. About a hundred years were needed to reach this point. Already in the early period, starting with the New Testament accounts of its institution, the original meal celebrated with the risen Lord by his friends was subject to pressure to interpret it. It was celebrated as *memoria*, as a commemoration and re-presentation of his passion. However, from the start of the second century the first signs of the idea that the community offers the Father its sacrificed Lord become apparent.[85] Christ becomes the Church's sacrifice, a development which, as we have seen (pp. 87ff. above), was encouraged by the charge of atheism brought by spokesmen for the Roman State. 1 Clement alreadt states that it is certified of the presbyters ousted from their ministry (*leitourgia*) that they had "ministered (*leitourgesantas*) blamelessly to the flock of Christ with humility" (44:3) and had "blamelessly and piously offered the gifts (*dora*)" (44:4). That *leitourgia* here does not have any meaning of ritual or worship but refers generally to the conduct of their

---

83. von Campenhausen (op. cit., p. 126) sees in ordination a "sacramental act" without however understanding the question itself differently.

84. von Campenhausen, "Die Anfänge des Priesterbegriffs in der alten Kirche," in his *Tradition und Leben*, Tübingen 1960, p. 276.

85. Cf. Rordorf, "Le sacrifice eucharistique," in *Liturgie, foi et vie des premiers chrétiens*, pp. 59-71.

office is undisputed, but what is in dispute is whether the term "gifts" refers also or principally to the eucharist.[86]

We have already seen that Justin Martyr uses expressions difficult to understand other than in the sense of the later Catholic teaching (pp. 65-67 above). Ignatius of Antioch may not make the sacrificial character of the eucharist explicit "but certainly hints at it". He himself would like to be poured out as a libation to God as long as there was still an altar (*thusiasterion*) ready (Rom. 2:2), whereby he clearly presupposes that the community gathers round such an object.[87] Clement of Alexandria nowhere discusses the sacraments as such, not even the eucharist, but from his occasional statements it is evident that for him the eucharist is at one and the same time prayer, meal, and sacrifice.[88] "It remains . . . to observe that Clement too links the idea of sacrifice with the eucharist."[89]

Finally there are the two Carthaginians, Tertullian and Cyprian. It is surprising that while Tertullian devoted a monograph to baptism and another to penance he did not write a separate treatise on the eucharist. Nevertheless, he is responsible for the greatest wealth of terminology applied to the eucharist. This includes the label *dominica sollemnia* and what subsequently became the classic term in the Church, the "sacrament of the eucharist" (*eucharistiae sacramentum*).[90] For Tertullian the essen-

---

86. A positive view is taken by Fischer (*Die Apostolischen Väter, griechisch und deutsch*) in his note on the passage ("above all" the eucharist), and an even more explicit line is taken by G. Blond, "Clément de Rome," in Rordorf and others, *L'eucharistie des premiers chrétiens*, Paris 1976, pp. 29-51, here 37-8. Andreas Lindemann (*Die Clemensbriefe*, Tübingen 1992) in his note on the passage doubts whether "we are dealing here with the earliest instance of the Catholic understanding of the Lord's supper."

87. Fischer, *op. cit.*, p. 131.

88. A. Méhat, "Clement d'Alexandrie" (in Rordorf and others, *op. cit.*, pp. 101-27, here 111-3).

89. Johannes Betz, *Eucharistie: in der Schrift und Patristik. Handbuch der Dogmengeschichte*, vol. 4, fasc. 4a, Freiburg-im-Breisgau 1979, p. 47.

90. For detailed treatment see V. Saxer, "Tertullien" (in Rordorf and others, *op. cit.*, pp. 129-50).

tial traits of the eucharist are the real presence and sacrifice.[91] Also noteworthy is that Tertullian writes of "reliable elders" (*probati seniores*) presiding at the eucharist.[92]

Cyprian of Carthage requires closer attention. As far as the eucharist is concerned he has the reputation of having emphasized its sacrificial character as strongly as possible. But prudence is demanded here. As is shown above all by his letter 63, written in the year 253, the eucharist for him is indeed *sacrificium, passio, oblatio*, but always in the traditional sense of *memoria, commemoratio*. It is *dominicae passionis et nostrae redemptionis sacramentum*, whereby *sacramentum* means the act of making sacramentally present.[93]

This does not, admittedly, make any difference to the fact that it is not the making present but the offering of Jesus' sacrifice that dominates the understanding of the eucharist of the third century. Where there is sacrifice, there, in the thinking of the time, there must also be a priest. "First of all there arises the idea of a special Christian service of worship and sacrifice which then at once brings in its train the corresponding idea of a special priestly vocation and class. . . . The idea of the priesthood follows, as has been said, the idea of ritual sacrifice."[94]

(5) The turning-point with Cyprian

For Cyprian, too, in the middle of the third century, ordination to the priesthood is not a sacrament.[95] Yet Cyprian personally, as well as his period (the middle of the third century), represents a significant turning-point for clerical structures. These change in three ways:

---

91. "Présence réelle et sacrifice véritable, ainsi se pourrait définir l'eucharistie de Tertullien" (*op. cit.*, p. 149).

92. *Op. cit.*, pp. 132, 147.

93. R. Johanny, "Cyprien de Carthage" (in Rordorf and others, *op. cit.*, pp. 151-75, here 161-4); cf. Richard Seagraves, *Pascentes cum disciplina. A Lexical Study of the Clergy in the Cyprianic Correspondence*, Fribourg 1993, p. 260. Cyprian is the oldest witness of the daily celebration of the eucharist.

94. von Campenhausen, *art. cit.*, pp. 174-6.

95. Seagraves, *op. cit.*, p. 105.

(1) Ministries that originally stood alongside bishops and presbyters and thus outside the clergy, such as teachers, were integrated into the hierarchy. They thus came under the supervision and control of the bishop.[96]

(2) From then on there was the possibility of rising from a lower ministry such as that of lector or reader, a ministry which until then had been a permanent one, to that of presbyter, if not indeed to bishop. Preliminary allocation to a lower rank could be for various reasons: youthfulness,[97] a probationary period, financial remuneration. The presbyter was on a different wage-scale.[98]

(3) This leads into the third point: ministry in the Church from then on became a full-time occupation and thereby a means of livelihood, while in earlier times it had been exercised on a part-time basis alongside a secular job. This meant that the Church developed into an organization that imitated the State.[99]

---

96. Examples of this development are to be found in D. Van Damme, "Bekenner und Lehrer. Bemerkungen zu zwei nichtordinierten Kirchenämtern in der Traditio Apostolica," in Cäcilia Fluck and others (ed.), *Divitiae Aegypti. Festschrift für Martin Krause*, Wiesbaden 1995, pp. 321-30.

97. Van Damme tells of "confessors" (Christians who steadfastly confessed their faith before the magistrate and who were in certain circumstances punished but not executed) whom Cyprian first made readers because of their youthful age, "in the expectation that they would later rise to the presbyterate" (art. cit., p. 326). A minimum age of twenty-five was demanded for municipal office (Elisabeth Herrmann, *Ecclesia in Re Publica. Die Entwicklung der Kirche von pseudostaatlicher zu staatlich inkorporierter Existenz* [note 2 above], p. 46; cf. note 99). An especially informative example of such an ascent is to be found in Cyprian's letter 55:8, where he reports of his colleague Cornelius: "What redounds to the praise of our dear Cornelius and recommends him to God and Christ and his Church as well as to all his fellow priests is that he did not suddenly attain the dignity of bishop," but reached the episcopate through all the stages after he had filled all the Church's ministries (*officia*) and had gained sufficient credit in the service of God.

98. "How much this wage was cannot be worked out. However we know that it must have been enough to cover living costs: Cyprian is very clear in insisting that priests were forbidden any ancillary occupation" (Van Damme, *art. cit.*, p. 327). The negative side-effects of the rise in social status and wages are well known and remain so today: ambition, money-grubbing, careerism.

99. How closely the Church brought its structures into line with the forms of the Roman constitution is impressively demonstrated by Herrmann (for

Hence it is no surprise that Cyprian puts forward a different picture both within the clergy and with regard to their relationship to the laity. Within the clergy the hierarchical organization of bishop, presbyter, and deacon has become a permanent arrangement. Two changes pregnant with consequences are to be noted from the situation found in the *Apostolic Tradition*:

(1) First, the status of the bishop is given the highest possible enhancement. For Cyprian *sacerdos* is always the bishop: he is the *sacerdos par excellence*.[100] He takes the place of Christ (*sacerdos vice Christi*).[101] As such he is responsible only to God.[102] The bishops are the successors of the apostles, the first bishops.[103] At the same time the class of presbyters attains its autonomy with Cyprian. Presbyters now have their own authority to preside over the eucharist and thus embody the Levitical priesthood of the Temple. The bishop's privileges (election, possession of the Spirit, forgiveness of sins, the eucharist) are handed on by him to the presbyters. He allocates the lots (*kleroi*) whose recipients thus become "clerics."[104] To these belong not only the upper ranks (bishop, presbyter, deacon) but also the lower orders such as acolytes and lectors.[105] Belonging to the clergy is no longer determined on the basis of the liturgy. A cleric is rather simply the holder of a Church office.

(2) This led to a deepening of the gulf between clergy and people. The binomial term *clerus—plebs* is common in Cyprian's

Cyprian in particular, *op. cit.*, pp. 42-52). For example, "*ordinare* is the technical term for permanent appointment in the imperial service" (p. 44). As far as Cyprian is concerned the same applies with regard to the Church hierarchy: "In the works of Cyprian, the verb *ordinare* and its associated noun *ordinatio* are not equivalent to the modern terms, to ordain and ordination" (Seagraves, op. cit., p. 28): in other words, they have nothing to do with "holy orders."

100. von Campenhausen, *Ecclesiastical Authority and Spiritual Power in the Church of the First Three Centuries*, p. 282 note 70; Seagraves, *op. cit.*, p. 68.

101. Seagraves, *op. cit.*, p. 68.

102. According to Seagraves (*op. cit.*, p. 3) Cyprian is "the first writer to maintain that a bishop is responsible only to God."

103. Seagraves, *op. cit.*, p. 27.

104. Faivre, *Ordonner la fraternité*, pp. 80-2.

105. Seagraves, *op. cit.*, p. 18.

writings.[106] Clerics and lay-people were clearly differentiated. When the bishop—or his presbyter—entered the church the congregation had to stand up.[107] So there was a shift from a priestly people to a people of the priests.[108]

A consequence of this development was that the laity were more and more condemned to passivity. A striking image of this is to be found in the Pseudo-Clementines, an early Christian romance (indeed, the first Christian novel) dating from the first half of the third century.[109] In this Peter gives Clement as his successor (*sic*) instructions about how he is to fulfil his office as well as about the duties of the presbyters, deacons, catechists, and the faithful. The Church is likened to a ship whose helmsman is Christ. The bishop is the lookout in the bows, the presbyters the sailors, the deacons the boatswains, the catechists the pursers. The "multitude of the brethren" (*i.e.* the faithful) are the passengers. They do not make the voyage: they are carried, and for better or worse they are at the mercy of the competence or otherwise of the crew. It is the image of a clerical Church as it has persisted through the centuries down to our own days.

The image is rounded off by the instruction that follows: "The passengers should remain steady, firmly seated in their places, so that they do not cause dangerous movements of the ship and make it list to one side through their disorderly behaviour."

---

106. "In the writings of St Cyprian one often finds the binomial term *clerus—plebs. Plebs* denotes the Christian people and *clerus* the group running the Church" (Vilela, *op. cit.*, p. 259).

107. von Campenhausen, *op. cit.*, p. 272.

108. ". . . du peuple de prêtres au peuple des prêtres," Faivre, *op. cit.*, p. 83.

109. A postulated original gave rise to the two extant versions which in fictional form narrate the journeys of Peter in Palestine and Syria and the biography of Clement of Rome. The romance is preceded by a pair of letters from Peter and Clement to James, bishop of Jerusalem. The quotation that follows comes from the second letter.

The significance of the Pseudo-Clementines for our knowledge of the early Church has been recognized for about two centuries. Recent research was opened up by Oscar Cullmann's monograph, *Le problème littéraire et historique du roman Pseudo-Clémentin*, Paris 1930. George Strecker (*Das Judenchristentum in den Pseudoklementinen*, Berlin ²1981) describes the present state of research, and the most recent study is J. Wehnert, "Abriß der Entstehungsgeschichte des Pseudoklementinischen Romans," in *Apokrypha* 3 (1992), pp. 211-35.

(6) The indelible character of the priesthood

A turning-point toward the emergence of the personal priest-hood was contributed by Augustine (354-430) "by distinguishing between the grace of the Holy Spirit, which can be lost, and an unlosable grace of the sacrament of order."[110] The sacrament of ordination persists even in the case of someone who loses his ecclesiastical office. "Even when someone is removed from office for some offence he retains the sacrament of the Lord he has once received."[111]

So for Augustine ordination cannot be repeated. It is indelibly imprinted on the priest and belongs to his character. That means that like the brand stamped on a slave, soldier or animal—termed *character*—it expresses an irrevocable relationship of property (slave-master, soldier-emperor, flock-shepherd). "The deserter does not bear the distinguishing mark of the deserter but of the commander. Similarly the baptized person carries permanently within himself or herself the sacrament of baptism and the ordained person the sacrament of ordination."[112]

---

110. Ludwig Ott, *Das Weihe-Sakrament. Handbuch der Dogmengeschichte*, vol. 4 fasc. 5, Freiburg-im-Breisgau 1969, p. 29.

111. Ott, *ibid.*

112. Ott, *op. cit.*, p. 30. Admittedly Augustine talks only occasionally of the priestly character but on the other hand very often of the character of baptism, though the raw material is present to be transferred to the priesthood (cf. E. Dassmann s.v. Character, *Augustinus-Lexikon* vol. 1, 1986-94, pp. 835-40). Augustine's lack of precision in ideas relating to this question is shown by the way he treats the concepts *sacramentum, sanctitas, consecratio, baptismus, ordinatio* as synonymous with *character*. Basically it is a question of a property relationship produced by baptism and permanent because baptism cannot be repeated. On the other hand, Augustine does not see it as a mark imprinted on the soul (cf. G. Bavaud in *Oeuvres de Saint-Augustin 29: Traités Anti-Donatistes, vol. II, de Baptismo libri VII*, Paris 1964, pp.. 581-2), so that it can be said that the doctrine of the priestly character is to be found in Augustine only in embryonic form ("*ce qui sera plus tarde la théologie du caractère est seulement en germe dans la doctrine augustinienne*," J. Pintard, *Le sacerdoce selon Saint Augustin*, 1960, p. 128). The doctrine of the indelible character such as we find in Thomas Aquinas is a construction of medieval theology that has dragged on through the centuries to the present day. Modern dogmatic theologians find it hard to define the nature and effect of this indelible sign. "In the Church's tradition this competence bestowed by ordination (*i.e.* to act in Christ's stead) is termed

We cannot therefore talk of a priesthood according to our contemporary understanding of it before the fifth century. "It is in any case certain that any traces of a *character indelibilis* or a 'sacrament' of priestly ordination cannot be demonstrated in the older Fathers, and when someone thinks they have found something of this kind it is a question of a misunderstanding. . . . The decisive change to a new, absolute conception of the priesthood took place around the turn from the fourth to the fifth century."[113]

This survey has shown that all ministries are the creation of the Church. None can be traced back to Jesus, not even that of the bishop, and least of all that of the priest. Hence the organization of these ministries remains even today in the hands of the Church. Above all the greatest variety reigned in the celebration of the eucharist. It was conducted by the entire community,[114] by the hosts of house churches, by prophets, teachers, elders, *episkopoi*, presbyters, and finally—from the fifth century onward—by sacramentally ordained priests. For nearly four centuries priestly ordination was not necessary for the enactment of the eucharist. Why should it be obligatory today?[115]

---

character indelibilis, indelible sign. It is indelible because it is grounded in Christ's steadfast promise and unswerving will to continue to mediate his work of salvation through the ministry of the ordained person" (G. Greshake, *Priester sein*, Freiburg im Breisgau 1982, p. 114).

113. von Campenhausen, *art. cit.* (note 84 above), p. 280. The evidence for an earlier starting-point presented by Lécuyer is not convincing. Proof that a sacrament that cannot be detected in the Church for four hundred years can have been instituted by Christ and is indeed a "fundamental office of the Church" (Kurt Koch, *Kirche der Laien? Plädoyer für die göttliche Würde der Laien in der Kirche*, Fribourg 1991, p. 12) must be left to the dogmatic theologians. As far as exegetes are concerned the matter has long been quite clear.

114. Hoffmann, *art. cit.* (note 49 above), p. 29, writes of presiding at the Lord's Supper: "In 1 Cor. 11 its conduct emerges as the business of the entire community. . . . The performers of the 'sacramental actions' are the 'we' of the community." On this basis the increasingly widespread usage, in congregations without a priest, of the whole congregation reciting the words of institution can be legitimized.

115. That awareness of this is growing is shown most recently by the conference of liturgists from the German-speaking world held from 23 to 27 September 1996, cf. *Herder-Korrespondenz* 50 (1996), pp. 641-4.

In conclusion

We can establish:

(1) In the Catholic Church there are two classes, clergy and laity, with different privileges, rights and duties. This structure does not correspond to what Jesus did and taught. Consequently it has not had a good effect in the history of the Church.

(2) The Second Vatican Council did indeed make a start at trying to bridge over the deep gulf between clergy and laity, but it did not do away with it. Even in the Council documents the laity appear as helpmates of the hierarchy, and they have no possibility of genuinely claiming the rights they are entitled to.

(3) Jesus rejected the Jewish priesthood and the worship based on blood sacrifice of his time. His relationship to the Temple and to the Temple worship conducted by priests was fragmentary. He proclaimed the downfall of the Jerusalem Temple and let it be understood that in its place he could not imagine any other temple. So it was the Jewish priesthood that delivered him to the cross.

(4) In none of his sayings did Jesus indicate that he wanted to see among his disciples a new priesthood and a new sacrificial worship. He himself was not a priest, nor was any of the Twelve, any of the apostles, nor even Paul. Still less should there be a new priesthood according to the other writings of the New Testament.

(5) Among his disciples Jesus did not want any distinction of class or rank. "You are all brothers," he stated (Matt. 23:8). So the first Christians regarded themselves and addressed each other as "brothers" and "sisters."

(6) In contradiction to this instruction of Jesus, a "hierarchy," a "sacred authority," was nevertheless formed in the third century. This had as a consequence the division of the faithful into two classes, clergy and laity, the "ordained" and the "people." The hierarchy claimed for itself the leadership of the congregations and above all of their worship. It expanded its power more and more. The laity were obliged to serve and to obey.

(7) The expansion of the Church throughout the world made forms of ministry necessary. As history shows, these could take on very different forms. All ministries, including that of the

bishop, are, however, things established by the Church. The Church is therefore able to maintain them, to change them, or to abolish them when conditions suggest this.

(8) Since the fifth century the celebration of the eucharist has demanded the co-operation of a sacramentally ordained priest. Since the fifth century also the idea has emerged that priestly ordination marks the recipient with an indelible sign or character. This doctrine was further developed by medieval theology and was made doctrinally binding by the Council of Trent in the sixteenth century.

(9) For four hundred years it was what we today would call lay people who presided at the eucharist. This shows that a sacramentally ordained priesthood is not necessary and can be justified neither biblically nor dogmatically.

(10) The condition for presiding at the eucharist should thus be not a form of consecration or ordination but a commission. This can be given to a man or a woman, whether married or unmarried. For both men and women the full ministry of the Church should be demanded, something that automatically includes authorization to conduct the eucharist.